Sweet Re

A play

Francis Durbridge

Samuel French — London
New York - Toronto - Hollywood

ISBN 0 573 01904 5

Please see page iv for further copyright information

SWEET REVENGE

First presented by Bill Kenwright at the Thorndike Theatre, Leatherhead, on 12th January 1993 with the following cast:

Judy Hilton	Abigail Thaw
Alan Wells	Ben Robertson
Marian Palmer	Lesley North
Ross Marquand	Richard Todd
Sam Kennedy	Peter Cartwright
Bill Yorke	David Baron
Fay Marquand	Meg Davies
Julian Kane	Hayward Morse
Norman Sanders	Christopher Birch
Maid	Jo McLaren-Clark

Directed by Val May
Designed by Geoffrey Scott

CHARACTERS

Alan Wells
Judy Hilton
Marian Palmer
Dr Ross Marquand
Dr Sam Kennedy
Bill Yorke
Fay Marquand
Julian Kane
Norman Sanders

The action takes place in the living-room of Dr Ross Marquand's house in the Thames Valley, near Marlow

Time — the present

Other plays by Francis Durbridge published by Samuel
French Ltd:

Deadly Nightcap
The Gentle Hook
House Guest
Murder with Love
The Small Hours
Suddenly at Home
A Touch of Danger

For Stephen and Nicholas

ACT I

SCENE 1

The living-room of Dr Ross Marquand's house in the Thames Valley, near Marlow. A late afternoon in June

It is a spacious and comfortable room. The furnishings are attractive without having been "created" by an interior decorator. There are several armchairs, a sofa, drinks cabinet, a centre table, and an impressive-looking desk bearing a telephone, notebooks, stationery, etc.

On the left a door leads to the doctor's consulting room; a second door leads to the kitchen. The entrance from the hall and front door is through an archway DR. *Large windows open on to a terrace which in turn leads down to the river*

When the CURTAIN *rises Alan Wells is sitting on the arm of the sofa just finishing a large scotch and soda. He is in his late twenties. His clothes are casual and there is a canvas holdall by the side of him*

There is a distinctly troubled expression on Alan's face as he finally finishes his drink and crosses to the cabinet. He is about to help himself to yet another drink when Judy Hilton, Dr Marquand's assistant, enters

Judy was formerly a nurse at one of the London hospitals. She is basically a friendly person but with some people she can be faintly officious. Alan is one of these people

Judy Sorry to have kept you. But I'm extremely busy this afternoon.
Alan Where is everybody? My sister appears to have vanished and there's no sign of Ross.
Judy He'll be back tomorrow. I'm afraid I don't know where Fay is. What is it you want, Alan? (*She looks at the glass he is holding*) Apart from free drinks ...

Alan hesistates, then puts the glass down and turns away from the cabinet

Alan I tried to get you on the phone last night.

Judy Yes, I know. I couldn't talk, I was about to dash up to London.

Alan Problems?

Judy There's always problems when you're dealing with builders. The way things are going, heaven only knows when we'll be back in Harley Street. Not that it worries the patients, they seem to prefer this neck of the woods. (*She crosses to the desk and puts down several letters she is holding*) Now, why do you want to see me? What is it you wish to talk about?

Alan I've got a couple of tickets for a first night and I was wondering whether you'd like to —

Judy (*stopping him*) I'm sorry. I can't make it.

Alan (*annoyed*) But you don't know when it is. I haven't told you. (*Pause*) I suppose if I were Bill Yorke it would be a different story?

Judy Yes. It probably would.

The telephone rings. Judy immediately turns her back to Alan and answers it

(*Into the phone*) This is Marlow seven-four. ... (*Surprised*) Why, hallo, Doctor! ... Where are you? ... We were not expecting you back until tomorrow. ... I'm afraid you can't, Fay's not here at the moment. ...

Alan Where is Ross? Where's he speaking from?

Judy (*to Alan*) He's at Heathrow. (*Into the phone*) I don't know where she is, Ross. ... Fay left the house early this morning and we haven't seen her since. (*A long pause. She listens intently*) Yes, I saw the report about Zarabell Four, it was in both *The Times* and the *Independent*. ... Several patients have telephoned and Dr Kennedy would like to see you as soon possible. ... He sounded very worried. ... What's that? ... Yes, I will. ... Yes, of course. ... (*She hangs up*)

Alan What's all that about Zarabell Four?

Judy It's a drug. A tranquillizer. Several people who have been taking it have died — quite suddenly.

Alan (*somewhat taken aback*) Really? Good Lord! I was on it for a time.

Judy You were?

Alan Yes. Ross prescribed it. It was last year whilst you were on holiday. I had a period when I couldn't sleep. I thought it was marvellous stuff. Used to put me out like a light.

Judy It does with some people. What were you on, the tablets or the liquid?

Alan The liquid. I used to take it in ginger ale. (*He grins*) Couldn't stand the sight of water.

Judy I'm surprised it wasn't scotch. (*She moves towards the consulting room*)

Alan (*anxiously*) Judy, don't go! I must talk to you.

Judy turns back

Is Julian Kane a friend of yours?

Judy (*staring at him*) Julian Kane? No. Why do you ask?

Alan He was here this afternoon. I caught sight of his car turning out of the drive.

Pause

Judy He came to see your sister ...

Alan To see Fay?

Judy Yes, but he was unlucky. She wasn't here.

Alan (*faintly alarmed*) Why Fay? Why did he want to see Fay?

Judy You'll have to ask your sister that question. (*She stares at him*) But why are *you* interested in Kane?

Alan (*hesitating; after a moment*) About nine months ago I was in a very difficult situation, moneywise ...

Judy Aren't you always in a difficult situation, moneywise?

Alan (*ignoring her remark*) To be frank, I'd been gambling and I was badly in debt. I just didn't know what to do. I couldn't turn to either of my sisters for help because they'd already baled me out, on more than one occasion ——

Judy Get to the point, Alan.

Alan One weekend I was feeling particularly desperate so I went down to Marian Palmer's place in the Cotswolds. I had it in mind to try and touch Marian for the money ——

Judy You must have been desperate! Mrs Palmer never stops telling her friends how broke she is.

Alan Unfortunately, Marian was giving a party and the house was full of people. It was impossible to talk to her. However, I met Julian. I knew of him, of course, and I'd heard the usual stories about him. To my surprise he seemed a very friendly person, not at all what I expected. We had a few drinks and I suddenly found myself telling him about the trouble I was in. To cut the story short ——

Judy He lent you the money?

Alan (*nodding*) Yes, and to start with he was perfectly friendly about the whole business; in fact, he never mentioned the money until about two months ago. Then he suddenly became difficult. He said the tax people were hounding him and he insisted on being repaid. I asked him to hold things over for a little while, but he threatened to speak to Fay about it. When I heard that he'd been here this afternoon ...

Judy You jumped to the conclusion he'd told your sister about the loan?

Alan Yes.

Judy Well, I can put your mind at rest. He hasn't.

Alan You're sure?

Judy I'm quite sure.

Alan is relieved, yet at the same time puzzled

Alan What makes you so sure?

Judy They've had other things to talk about.

Alan And what does that mean?

Judy hesitates, then avoids the question by giving a little shrug

What are you suggesting?

Judy I'm not suggesting anything.

Alan But you are!

Judy (*after a short pause*) Fay's a wealthy woman. Both she and Diana inherited a fortune from your uncle.

Alan I'm acutely aware of that! But what's that got to do with Kane?

Judy (*quietly, yet there's no mistaking the contempt in her voice*) Kane's not just a womanizer, he's an opportunist, and your sister's fallen for him.

Alan (*stunned*) I don't believe this!

Judy It's true.

Alan (*incredulously*) Why, Fay adores Ross!

There is an awkward moment. In spite of his protest, Alan is distinctly shaken

Are you serious, Judy?

Judy Yes, I'm serious.

Pause

Alan (*worried*) Does Ross know?
Judy No. Not yet.
Alan (*fervently*) Well, one thing's for certain! Whatever happens, Fay will never leave him. I know my sister!
Judy But you don't know Julian. You only think you do.
Alan (*obviously surprised by her remark*) Do you know him, Judy?

Pause

Judy A friend of mine was happily married, devoted to his wife. His wife met Julian and in next to no time there was a separation. My friend was heartbroken. Still is, I'm afraid. (*Pause*) Yes, I've met Julian Kane. Once. It was a long time ago, before he became famous. I doubt whether he remembers me. (*She moves away*)

Voices are heard in the hall

After a moment Marian Palmer enters. She is in her early forties and runs a boutique in Beauchamp Place

Marian (*exasperated*) Alan! Where on earth is Fay?
Judy I'm afraid Mrs Marquand's out at the moment, Mrs Palmer.
Marian (*to Alan, ignoring Judy*) Where is she, Alan? I've been trying to get in touch with her for days! I'm beginning to think she's avoiding me.
Alan Of course she's not avoiding you! An old friend like you, Marian!
Marian (*unaware of his sarcasm*) She hasn't been near the boutique and I simply must talk to her. The regatta's in ten days' time and I haven't the faintest idea what the arrangements are or what she'll be wearing.
Alan (*surprised*) The regatta? (*He looks at Judy*) I thought there wasn't going to be one this year. Ross swore he was finished with all that razzmatazz.
Judy Yes, I know, but there was such an uproar. The local shopkeepers complained and the charity people were up in arms.
Marian I'll bet they were! We raised nearly forty thousand pounds for them last year.
Alan We, Marian?

Marian Darling, I worked my fingers to the bone, you know that. I must have decorated every quare inch of *Spring Fever*.
Alan *Spring Fever*?
Marian Ross's cabin cruiser, or launch, or whatever.
Alan *Spring Tide*, not *Fever*.
Marian All right, darling, have it your own way. *Spring Tide*.
Judy (*smiling*) I'll tell Fay you called, Mrs Palmer.
Marian Yes, do that.

Judy exits into the consulting room

Why does she insits on calling me Mrs Palmer? She calls Ross, "Ross" and Fay, "Fay". Why on earth doesn't she call me Marian and have done with it? She's always so damned supercilious.
Alan Not always, Marian. By the way, I bumped into your husband last weekend.
Marian Did you? That must have made your day. (*Contemptuously*) The mean little devil!
Alan (*amused*) Mean? Come off it, Marian! He gave you the flat, he bought you a house in the country, and he set you up in business. What more did you expect?
Marian He "set me up" all right, and he knew exactly what he was doing. I'm now tied to that blasted boutique from morning till night. Anyway, you'll be glad to know I've capitulated. I've decided to give him a divorce after all. So perhaps he'll be more generous in future.
Alan I thought you were dead against a divorce?
Marian I was, but — (*hesitantly*) I had lunch with his father and he talked me into it.
Alan I sometimes think you should have married his father.
Marian You're not the only one. (*Irritated*) Look — where is Fay, Alan? And how long will she be?
Alan I haven't the faintest idea.
Marian Is there any point in my staying, do you think?
Alan It's entirely up to you.
Marian (*after a moment's consideration*) Well, if you're lucky enough to set eyes on her, tell her to phone me. I shall be in all evening.
Alan (*kissing her goodbye*) I'll do that.

Marian moves towards the hall

(*Stopping her; quietly*) Oh — and Marian.

She turns

I'm glad you're giving your husband a divorce.
Marian I'm glad you're glad.
Alan But don't think I've swallowed that story about his father. My bet is, you've got another reason.

She stares at him for a brief moment

Marian There's always another reason, darling. For practically everything.

She exits

After Marian has departed, Alan picks up his bag and moves towards the consulting room. He obviously intends to have another word with Judy, but when he gets near the door he suddenly has second thoughts, changes his mind, and returns to the drinks cabinet. With one eye on the consulting room door, he quickly searches the cabinet for an unopened bottle of scotch, finally discovers one, examines the label, then puts the bottle in his hold-all

He turns away from the cabinet and heads towards the open window as the Lights fade

SCENE 2

The same day. Ten o'clock at night

The room is in darkness except for the light from a standard lamp near the desk. A vase of lovely flowers has been placed on the table. The front doorbell is ringing

Ross Marquand is sitting at the desk trying to compose a difficult letter. Ross, a successful consultant, is not conventionally good-looking but he has a likeable personality and, when the occasion calls for it, an unmistakable air of authority

When the doorbell stops ringing, Ross rises and exits to the hall

After a moment he enters with Dr Sam Kennedy. Sam is a hard-working, conscientious GP. He carries a briefcase

Ross Hallo, Sam! Good of you to drop in at this time of night.

Sam Good of you to see me, Ross. I appreciate it. Sorry I couldn't make it earlier.

Ross That's all right.

Sam I've only just left the hospital and I've still a couple of calls to make. A GP's work in never done these days, I'm afraid.

Ross (*smiling*) I'm sure you're right. But no cracks about consultants. Not at this time of night. Put your things down and let me get you a drink.

Sam No, I won't have a drink, if you don't mind.

Ross Well — sit down, Sam.

Sam looks about him, hesitates, then decides to sit on the sofa. Ross returns to his chair at the desk and swivels it round so that he faces Sam

Ross You're worried, my friend?

Sam Yes, I am.

Ross It's Liz, I take it?

Sam No, it's nothing to do with Liz. I'm worried about her, of course. Very worried — and my wife's in a terrible state, poor darling. Hardly ever moves away from the phone. But that's not why I wanted to see you. It's about Zarabell Four. Do you recall a young man called Brian Haskins? I referred him to you a couple of months back?

Ross Yes, of course. He's in the City. Works for one of the Investment Houses.

Sam (*nodding*) You confirmed my diagnosis and suggested we put him on a course of Zarabell.

Ross That's right.

Sam You wrote me to that effect.

Ross Yes, I'm sure I did. (*A shade puzzled*) What is it, Sam?

Sam He had a heart attack this morning whilst on his way to the office. He's in intensive care.

Ross Oh! I'm sorry to hear that.

Sam I doubt whether he's going to make it, Ross. (*Perturbed*) However, the point is — his brother telephoned me this afternoon and said, in no uncertain terms, that I was to blame for the heart attack ...

Ross Did he, indeed?

Sam He claims I ought never to have put him on Zarabell.

Ross And what did you say, Sam?

Sam I said Brian had seen a consultant and had there been any suggestion of a heart condition the drug would never have been prescribed. (*He shakes his head*) But he wasn't happy. Not at all happy. Mark my words, Ross, if the worst does happen, he'll make trouble.

Ross gazes at him for a second or two

Ross Sam, do you want my opinion? My honest opinion?

Sam Yes, of course! That's why I'm here.

Ross You're desperately worried about your daughter, which is understandable of course, but it's no help when it comes to other problems. You're jumping the gun over Zarabell Four. First of all, Brian Haskins may not die. Secondly, if he does, and his brother gets difficult, really difficult, then refer him to me. I prescribed Zarabell, not you, Sam. So it's my problem — not yours. Now put this business out of your mind. You've got more than enough to worry about at the moment.

Sam (*obviously relieved*) Thank you, Ross.

Pause

Ross I take it the Liz situation is the same? You haven't heard from her?

Sam No — it's just the same. And it's over seven weeks since she disappeared. Disappeared! My God, how I hate that word! And yet I keep on using it.

Ross What do the police say?

Sam They say very little. They've questioned her friends of course, and they've talked to her boss at the Barbican, but they don't seem to have come up with anything.

Ross What about the young man she was living with?

Sam Gordon? That was over some time back. Liz broke it off and moved into a bedsitter in Earls Court.

Ross He seemed a pleasant young man. Both Fay and I liked him.

Sam (*nodding*) He's a delightful person. We were quite upset when Liz left him. The poor devil was in a no-win situation. He wanted to marry Liz, but the silly girl just wouldn't hear of it. (*Pause*) It's a funny thing, Ross. Although I'm worried, desperately worried, I still have the feeling ... (*he hesitates*)

Ross Go on, Sam.

Sam I still have the feeling that she's all right and that nothing very terrible has happened to her. For the life of me, I don't know why I should think that. Every time I pick up a newspaper there's a story about some poor girl having been raped or murdered.

Ross Who was the last person to see Liz, do you know?

Sam A colleague of hers at the Barbican. She told the police she caught sight of Liz coming out of a disco on Tottenham Court Road.

Ross When was this?

Sam Oh — must be four or five weeks ago.

Ross rises

Ross Well, if there's anything I can do to help ...

Sam There's nothing you can do. (*He gets up and prepares to leave*) There's nothing anyone can do at the moment. (*At they move towards the hall*) I'll keep you posted about Haskins.

Ross Yes, please do that. I'll probably have a word with the hospital myself tomorrow morning. (*With a friendly gesture*) See you at the regatta, Sam.

Sam Yes. I'm very much looking forward to it.

As they reach the hall Judy enters from the terrace with Bill Yorke. Bill is quite a bit older than Judy and has a slightly old-fashioned air about him. This enables him to be frequently underrated

Ross (*turning*) Hallo, Bill! Judy ...

Bill Good-evening, Ross.

Ross (*pleased to see him*) What have you been doing with yourself, Bill? It's a long time ...

Bill Yes, I'm afraid it is. Too long.

Judy (*to Ross*) What time did you get home?

Ross Oh — about half past six, seven o'clock.

Judy We must have just missed each other. (*She smiles at Sam*) Good-evening, Doctor.

Sam Hallo, Judy. (*To Bill*) Nice to see you again, Bill. Are you well?

Bill Yes, I'm fine, thank you.

Sam (*to Ross*) He's just renovated that wonderful boat of his ...

Ross *Toymaker*.

Sam That's right. *Toymaker*. Looks fabulous. (*To Bill*) That was a memorable day we spent with you last month, Bill. That friend of mine's been talking of buying a boat ever since. (*To Judy*) My idea of Heaven would be to spend the rest of my life messing about on a boat like *Toymaker*.

They laugh

Ross See you later, Bill.

Sam nods to Bill and smiles at Judy before going out into the hall with Ross

Pause

Bill I suppose I'd better be making a move too.
Judy There's no hurry.

Pause

Bill Super film tonight.
Judy Er — yes. You like musicals, don't you, Bill?
Bill Yes, I do. Very much. Love all the Fred Astaire movies. Got the lot on video. Super. (*Pause*) Ross looks well. What was he doing in Scotland?
Judy A group of Scottish doctors have opened a clinc, chiefly for young drug addicts. Ross became involved and he goes up there every so often.
Bill Would that be The New Day Clinic?
Judy That's right.
Bill I heard someone talking about it on the radio. They're doing a super job from all accounts. (*After a tiny pause*) Quite a workaholic, our Ross.
Judy You don't exactly fight shy of work, do you, Bill?
Bill Well — you could say that, I suppose. Incidentally, Judy, I don't think you've seen our workshop. I'd love to show it to you sometime.
Judy (*with an apologetic little laugh*) I don't even know what you make.
Bill Toys.
Judy Toys?
Bill Yes. You sound surprised. (*He chuckles*) Hence *Toymaker*.
Judy Oh! Oh, I see. (*Amused*) That never occured to me! What sort of toys do you make, Bill?

Bill All sorts. Our best seller is a lion called Leopold. He wears a Stetson, cowboy boots, and a very loud checked shirt. You must have seen him in the shops.

Judy Leopold? Yes, of course! He's lovely.

Bill He sells at thirty-four ninety-nine, complete with an extra pair of boots and a couple of shirts. But for you, my dear, we'll make a special offer.

Judy smiles. There is a pause, then she suddenly becomes aware of the fact that he is looking at her intently

There's something I want to ask you, Judy.

Judy Yes, Bill?

Bill I — I probably gave you that impression at dinner?

Judy You talked about the South of France most of the time.

Bill Did I? (*He hesitates*) Yes. Yes, I suppose I did. I've just bought a house down there, at Menton. It overlooks the harbour. I — I think you'd like it, Judy.

Judy I'm sure I would.

Bill clears his throat

Bill I'm asking you to marry me, Judy.

Judy (*quietly*) I rather thought you were.

An appreciable pause

Bill The answer's no?

Judy I'm afraid it is, Bill. I'm sorry. (*A brief silence*) I really am sorry.

Bill Well — not to worry. It's been a super evening and I've enjoyed every minute of it. (*He moves to Judy and gently kisses her*) Now, I must go. I won't embarrass you further.

Judy I'm not embarrassed. I'm flattered. (*After a slightly awkward pause*) Bill, do you remember that afternoon, about six months ago when you took a party of us down the river?

Bill Yes.

Judy It started to rain and we sat talking, just the two of us, under an umbrella ...

Bill (*puzzled*) Yes, I remember.

Judy You told me that you were once engaged to a girl called Norma Craig ...
Bill Did I?
Judy Yes.

Pause

Bill Well?
Judy You never told me what happened.

Pause

Bill (*quite simply, as he turns away from her*) She died. (*A brief hesitation*) I'll be off, Judy. I've got a meeting early tomorrow morning. Goodnight, my dear.

He exits on to the terrace

Judy is staring after Bill, puzzled by his somewhat abrupt departure, when Ross enters. He is surprised to find Judy on her own

Ross Bill's not here?
Judy No. You've just missed him.
Ross Oh! I was hoping to have a nightcap.
Judy (*not quite sure what to say*) He's only just this minute left.

Ross looks at her and realizes that she too is puzzled by Bill's departure

(*Making conversation*) How are things at the clinic?
Ross Things are going well. Very well, I'm glad to say.
Judy I wish I could say the same about Harley Street. It'll be some little time I'm afraid before our rooms are ready.
Ross Well, not to worry. There's nothing we can do. The more you chase the builders the longer the hold-up. (*He looks at his watch*) Judy, what the devil's happened to Fay?
Judy She had an appointment at the hairdresser's first thing the morning. That's all I know. (*Deliberately changing the subject*) Before I forget, you were right about Ashley Richardson. Both the x-ray and the tests were negative. There's nothing for him to worry about.

Ross Oh, I'm delighted to hear that. Does he know?

Judy No. Since he's a friend of yours I thought you'd like to tell him yourself.

Ross I'll phone him first thing tomorrow morning. He'll be relieved. My God, he's a worrier, that man.

Judy I'd be a worrier if I had to earn my living as a private eye.

Ross (*amused*) A private eye?

Judy Well, if he's not a private eye, what is he? He's no longer with Scotland Yard.

Ross Haven't you seen his notepaper? He's a personal research consultant.

There is the noise of a door closing and both Ross and Judy turn towards the hall

After a slight pause Fay Marquand enters. She is a good-looking woman, somewhat younger than her husband. She wears a smart suit and carries a scarf which she has obviously just removed. She gives a sudden start of surprise on seeing Ross

Fay Why, Ross! I thought you were coming back tomorrow.

Ross I was, but I'd finished at the clinic, so I made a dash to the airport and managed to catch the last plane.

Fay You should have telephoned. I'd have met you.

Ross I did, but you were out.

Ross is quietly looking at Fay. Judy is acutely aware of this

Judy I'll — I'll say good-night, Fay.

Fay Good-night, Judy.

Ross Good-night.

Judy Good-night, Ross.

Judy exits

After an uncertain pause, Fay suddenly notices the flowers

Fay What beautiful flowers! Did you get them, Ross?

Ross Yes.

Fay They're lovely. I adore yellow roses.

Ross I know. There's some more in the breakfast room.

Pause

Ross I wondered what had happened to you. I telephoned several of our friends and no-one seemed to know where you were or what you were doing. I even spoke to Marian.
Fay You must have been worried. And what did Marian have to say?
Ross She seems to think you've been avoiding her.
Fay I'm afraid I have.
Ross Oh ... (*Pause*) Would you like some coffee?
Fay No, I don't think so, thank you.
Ross You're sure?
Fay Yes, I'm quite sure.
Ross Have you eaten?
Fay Yes. I — I went to Pinellio's.
Ross (*astonished*) Pinellio's? Good heavens, it must be years since we went to Pinellio's. Whatever made you go there?
Fay I — just felt like it.
Ross Who did you go with?
Fay I didn't go with anyone.
Ross (*puzzled*) You went on your own?
Fay Yes. (*Hesitantly*) The place has changed a great deal, I'm afraid.
Ross I imagine it has.
Fay They've got a happy hour now, and there's pop music playing the whole time.

Pause. Fay moves away from him and crosses to the table. She stands for a little while looking down at the flowers

Ross (*concerned*) What is it, Fay? What is it you want to tell me?
Fay (*turning to face him*) I'm in love with someone else, Ross.

Ross stares at her, totally stunned

I've been wanting to tell you this for days. But I've been frightened, and worried, and nearly always unhappy. I tried to fight it, Ross! Please believe that! That's why I went to Pinellio's. I thought, if I could recall certain things, little incidents from the past, then ... maybe ...

There is a brief, uncomfortable silence

Ross You'd better tell me what happened. Do I know this man? Have we met?

Fay No, but you must have heard of him. He's a musician. His name's Julian Kane.

Ross (*surprised*) Julian Kane? The conductor?

Fay Yes.

Ross (*after a tiny pause*) Yes, I've heard of him.

Fay (*a shade suspicious*) What have you heard? Has Marian been talking to you about him?

Ross Marian? No.

Fay Or Alan?

Ross No-one's been talking to me!

Fay But you've heard the stories, is that it?

Ross What stories? (*From now on his manner becomes increasingly tense*)

Fay There are stories about Julian. Dreadful stories. But they're not true, believe me they're not! He's gentle and kind, and always very honest.

Ross Well, I'm all for honesty, you know that. But you still haven't told me what happened.

Fay We met about five weeks ago whilst you were in Scotland. Marian took me to a concert at the Barbican. She's by way of being a friend of Julian's. Afterwards we stayed behind for drinks and she introduced me to him ...

Ross Go on ...

Fay The next day, by sheer coincidence, I bumped into him in the West End. We stood talking and, finally, he asked me to have dinner with him ...

Ross And this happened five weeks ago?

Fay Yes.

Ross Then why haven't you told me about this before now? (*With an edge of anger in his voice*) What were you frightened of? A ragbag of platitudes? A cosy little lecture?

Fay stares at him, startled by the sudden hostility

Fay (*softly; almost frightened*) Ross, please ...

Ross (*bitterly*) What do you mean — "Ross, please"?

Fay I'd like to talk about this sensibly. Without either of us losing our temper.

Ross Would you, Fay?

Fay Yes, darling ...

Ross Well, I'm sorry to disappoint you, but I don't feel very sensible at the moment. Oh, I know how I should feel! I've read about this situation many, many times. The wife who's out of her depth and the quiet, sympathetic husband. Well, I don't feel sympathetic! I feel bloody angry, if you must know! However, I'm a practical person, I daresay you've realized that by now. So — what is it you want? What is it you want me to do?

Fay (*miserably; stumbling*) I — I don't know. I just don't know. Except that ... I'd like you to meet Julian. I'd like you to talk to him ...

Ross Why? Why in God's name should I do that? There's nothing to be gained by our meeting. Absolutely nothing!

Fay (*brokenly*) Very well ...

Pause

Ross (*relenting somewhat*) However, if that's what you want, I'll think about it. (*Pause*) I can't be fairer than that, can I?

Fay No, Ross. You can't be fairer than that.

Ross Now, if you'll excuse me, it's getting late and I have an important letter I must write before tomorrow morning. (*He turns somewhat abruptly and crosses to the desk*)

Fay is deeply hurt and after a momentary hesitation, she exits into the hall

There is a pause before Ross sits at the desk, picks up his pen, and once again looks at the letter. But his thoughts are on Fay and eventually, in anger and frustration, he tosses the pen across the desk and buries his head in his hands. He is no longer sure, in his own mind, that he has handled the situation with Fay as it should have been handled. He sits like this for some little time, then slowly rises

He paces the room, an unmistakable expression of despair on his face. A sudden thought occurs to him. He stops dead, giving the thought consideration. Reaching a decision, he crosses to the phone and dials a number

A distinct pause

(*Into the phone*) Ashley Richardson? ... Dr Marquand ... Yes, I have —
and it's good news. ... I told you not to worry, dear boy. ... Yes, we had
the report this afternoon. Couldn't have been better. ... One hundred per
cent. ... Now just put it out of your mind and stop worrying. ... Yes, of
course! ... Yes, of course I will. ... And Ashley, I wonder if you would
do something for me? ... It's rather an unusual request and I can't tell you
why I'm making it — not at the moment. ... I'd like you to find out
everything you possibly can about a man called Julian Kane ...

The Lights fade

Scene 3

The same. Two days later at four o'clock in the afternoon

*Ross is at the cabinet preparing a drink for himself. He is on edge and is
showing unmistakable signs of stress. He has mixed the drink and is
actually raising the glass when it dawns on him that he is being stupid, that
it is far too early in the day for him to start drinking. With a muttered
"What the hell am I doing?", he puts the glass down and pushes it out of
reach*

*Judy enters from the consulting room and, unnoticed by Ross, stands
quietly watching him. She is carrying several letters and a document*

Ross suddenly becomes aware of her presence

Judy Are you all right?
Ross Yes, of course I'm all right!
Judy Don't forget you've got two more appointments and then there's the
   hospital ——
Ross When did I last overlook an appointment?
Judy It's not that, Ross. It's just that ...
Ross (*stopping her*) I know! I know! You don't have to tell me. (*Pause*)
   I'm sorry, my dear. (*Turning away from the cabinet*) Was I very bad with
   that little woman from Henley?
Judy On the contrary. She told me she felt much better after she'd seen
   you. Quite relieved, in fact.
Ross Well, that's something, I suppose. If it wasn't for the scare we're
   having I'd have put her on Zarabell.

Judy Yes, I realized that. Incidentally, I checked our supply. We have nine phials.

Ross Nine? Is that all?

Judy Yes.

Ross You'd better let me have them. (*After a brief silence*) You know about Fay, I take it?

Judy Yes, I know.

Ross She told you?

Judy (*shaking her head*) No; she didn't tell me. She didn't have to. I've been aware of the situation for some time now.

Ross stares at her

One day last week, when we were in Harley Street, I made up my mind to tell you about Kane.

Ross Why didn't you?

Judy I suddenly became nervous. So I took the easy way out. I told myself you wouldn't believe me and in any case it was none of my business. (*After a sympathetic pause*) What happened, Ross?

Ross There was a scene and I didn't handle it very well, I'm afraid. I was out of my depth and in the end I lost my temper. I've regretted it ever since. (*Tense, yet adamant*) But I've made up my mind, Judy! I'm not going to lose Fay! I'm not going to let a crazy infatuation ruin her life, to say nothing of my own. (*Pause*) Fay wants me to see Kane. To talk to him.

Judy (*with a little nod*) You have to see him eventually. Whether you want to or not. It's inevitable, Ross.

Ross makes no comment

Where is Fay? I've been wanting to have a word with her. I've had the regatta secretary on the phone twice this afternoon.

Ross She's spending the day with her sister. She'll be back this evening.

Judy nods and hands him the letters and document

Judy These are the Harley Street letters and the copy of the lease. You said you wanted to see them.

Ross (*taking the papers*) Thank you.

Judy watches him, obviously concerned, then she moves towards the consulting room. As she does so, voices are heard. Both Ross and Judy turn and look towards the hall

See who that is, Judy.

Judy exits into the hall

Ross looks at the document

Judy re-enters

Judy Dr Kennedy's here.
Ross (*surprised*) Sam?
Judy He'd very much like to see you, Ross.
Ross Yes. Yes, of course.

Ross crosses towards the hall as Judy goes into the consulting room

Come along in, Sam!

Sam enters

Sam I'd very much like to have a word with you, Ross. (*Hesitantly*) But, if it's a difficult moment, please say so.
Ross It isn't at all difficult. My next appointment isn't until five o'clock. Sit down, Sam.

Sam crosses to one of the armchairs

You look worried. What's the problem? Haskins?
Sam Haskins? No, no, it's nothing to do with Brian Haskins. As a matter of fact, he's getting better. He's already out of intensive care and there's talk of them discharging him at the end of the week.
Ross (*sitting on the arm of the sofa*) I'm relieved to hear that. And I'm quite sure you are.
Sam Yes, I'm very relieved.

Ross studies him for a moment

Ross Well, I must say, you don't look very relieved. On the contrary, you look as if doom is just about to descend. What is it, Sam?

Sam It's Liz.

Ross You still haven't heard from her?

Sam Yes, we've heard from her. In fact, she's home. The police picked her up late last night.

Ross Well — that's good news, surely.

Sam Yes, it is, but ...

Ross But, what? (*Pause*) Come on, Sam. If you need my help, which you obviously do, you must confide in me.

Sam The police raided a club in Soho. They questioned half a dozen girls. Liz was one of them.

Ross In Soho? What sort of a club?

Sam Heaven only knows!

Ross Was she working there?

Sam I think she must have been. A police sergeant recognized her, thank God, and brought her home. (*Pause*) She's on heroin, Ross.

Ross Oh! (*Pause*) I rather imagined something like that might have happened. Well — I'll help you in any way I can, Sam. I'm very fond of Liz.

Sam I know that. And she's fond of you, Ross.

Ross But first, let me have the whole story.

Sam We don't know the whole story. Janet and I are completely in the dark. We sat up all night talking about her. In the end, we were more confused than ever.

Ross What does Liz have to say?

Sam We can't get anything out of her. She flatly refuses to talk about the past.

Ross And the ex-boyfriend? Have you talked to Gordon?

Sam He's shattered. Completely shattered. He swears he hadn't the slightest idea she was on drugs.

Ross Do you believe him?

Sam Yes. Yes, I do. And so does Janet.

Pause. Ross rises

Ross I'm interested in a clinic, Sam. It's in Scotland, near Perth ...

Sam Yes, I know. And to be honest with you, Ross — that's why I'm here. Would it be possible for Liz to spend some time up there? Both my wife and I feel we'd like to get her away from London. As far away as possible.

Ross I can well understand that. (*Pause*) The clinic's pretty full at the moment, but — supposing I can find a place for her — would she go, do you think?

Sam I think Janet and I could talk her into it. We'd certainly try.

Ross Then I'll see what I can do.

Sam rises

There's a chap at the clinic called Lestrade. Tom Lestrade. He's fantastic with young people. Extraordinary man. Every other word is a four-letter word, but he works miracles. I'll talk to him about Liz.

Sam Thank you, Ross. I — I just don't know what to say.

Ross You don't have to say anything. Just stop worrying! And tell Janet to do the same.

They move toward the hall

I'll phone you tonight. Without fail, I promise.

Sam gives a grateful nod and exits

Ross looks at his watch, collects his thoughts for a moment, then crosses to the phone

He is dialling when Sam re-enters with Marian

Sam You've got a visitor, Ross.

Ross (*replacing the phone; surprised*) Why, hallo, Marian!

Sam (*smiling at Marian*) Nice talking to you again, Mrs Palmer. Hope to see you at the regatta.

Marian Yes. Yes, indeed. I'm sure we're all looking forward to it.

Sam exits

(*Staring after Sam*) Who is that? Do I know him?

Ross (*smiling*) Yes, you've met him. Dr Kennedy. Mad on boats and can't even afford a dinghy, poor devil.

Marian Yes, of course! Stupid of me! Ross, do forgive, bursting in on you like this. But it is important. It really is, darling.

Ross (*indicating the sofa*) Well, if it's that important, you'd better sit down.

Marian hesitates, then moves to the sofa

(*Studying her*) Aren't you well, Marian?

Marian Yes, I'm fine. It's just that ... I'm terribly worried ...

Ross Oh? What is it you're worried about?

Marian It's very difficult, Ross. I — I don't quite know where to begin. I thought of talking to Alan. I very nearly did, then I changed my mind. (*A brief, awkward silence*) ... I've known Fay a long time, Ross. We're very old friends.

Ross Yes, Marian.

Marian We were at school together.

Ross Yes, Marian.

Pause

Marian Ross, don't you think it might be a good idea if you and Fay went away for a little while? Just the two of you. It's ages since the pair of you had a holiday.

Ross stares at Marian who becomes increasingly embarrassed

Ross Marian, why don't you come straight out with it? Why don't you tell me about Julian Kane?

Marian (*completely taken aback*) You know about Julian?

Ross Yes, I know.

Marian Fay's in love — or thinks she's in love — with him.

Ross nods

Well?

Ross Well, what, Marian?

Marian (*rising*) Well, for God's sake! What are you going to do about it?

Ross What would you suggest I do?

Marian I've told you! You must take her away! As soon as possible!

Ross And you think that would solve the problem?

Marian I don't know whether it would solve it or not! All I know is ... (*She stops, looking at him earnestly*) Do you know Julian? Have you met him?

Ross No.

Marian Well — whatever you do, don't underrate him.

Ross Why should I underrate him? (*Pause*) You appear to be remarkably well-informed about Mr Kane. How did that come about, Marian?

Pause

Marian Let's just say I'm well-informed and leave it at that. (*Pause*) Do you remember a young actress called Sylvia Cartwright?

Ross No. Should I remember her?

Marian She had an affair with Julian and became pregnant. He talked the poor girl into an abortion which she didn't want and — she died.

Ross Have you told Fay this?

Marian No.

Ross Why not? (*Pause*) Don't you think you ought to tell her?

Marian She wouldn't believe me. Whatever I said about Julian she just wouldn't believe me.

Pause

Ross Well — thank you for coming. It can't have been easy for you.

Marian It wasn't. But Fay's my best friend, Ross, so I felt it only fair that I should talk to you.

Judy enters. She is holding a small cardboard box

Judy Oh, I beg your pardon, I thought ——

Ross That's all right. Marian's just leaving.

Judy Good-afternoon, Mrs Palmer.

Marian give Judy a brief nod and exits with Ross

Judy crosses to the desk, looks at the box she is holding, then puts it down

Ross re-enters

I've brought you the Zarabell. I was right. We've nine phials left, that's all.

Ross Thank you. We'd better keep them in here.

The phone rings. Judy answers it

Judy (*into the phone*) Yes, it is. ... Who wants Dr Marquand? ... Oh, just a minute! (*To Ross*) It's Ashley Richardson.

Ross Oh! (*He takes the phone from her but makes no attempt to speak*)

Judy looks at him, surprised by the fact that he obviously doesn't wish her to hear the conversation

Thank you, Judy.

She exits

Pause

(*Into the phone*) Hallo, Ashley! Have you any news?... Yes, I'm listening. ... Go on, Ashley. ... Was the girl's name Cartwright? ... (*Quietly*) Yes, I've heard of her. ... Are you sure Kane was involved?... Absolutely sure? ... I see. ... Yes, I understand. I understand completely. ... Thank you, Ashley, I'm very grateful. ... (*Surprised*) I'm sorry! What's that?... When did he have the heart attack, do you know? ... Which hospital? ... No! No, don't do that, it's not necessary. ... You've been most helpful, Ashley, and I appreciate it. See you soon, I hope. (*He hangs up*)

Ross stands staring down at the box of Zarabell, his thoughts on the conversation he has had with Ashley Richardson. After a moment he picks up the box, opens it, and takes out a single phial of Zarabell. He holds the phial in his hand, staring at it. There is a strange look on his face. It is almost as if he is agonizing over something. Finally, he makes a decision, puts the phial down, picks up the phone, and dials

Pause

(*Into the phone; trying to control the tenseness in his voice*) Diana? ... It's Ross. Could I have a word with Fay? ... Thank you, Diana. ... Fay,

I'm awfully sorry about the other night. I behaved badly, I'm afraid. ...
No, darling, please listen to me! I've decided to see Julian. ... No, really!
I mean it! I want to see him and I've had an idea, Fay. Why don't I invite
him down here, for the regatta? I'm sure that would make things easier
for you, for all of us, in fact. ... No, seriously, my dear, I've given this
matter thought and I'd very much like to do that. ... All right, Fay, we'll
talk about it tonight. (*He hangs up*)

*There is a tense silence. He slowly picks up the phial again. He stares at
the phial of Zarabell Four as the Lights fade*

SCENE 4

Ten days later. Morning

*Through the open window we can see that although the sun is shining,
there is the suggestion of gathering clouds. From the terrace there is the
sound of voices and of a party in progress*

*As Judy comes out of the consulting room, Ross appears from the terrace.
They are both wearing clothes suitable for a day on the river*

Ross Fay wants to know if you've spoken to Mellow House about another
marquee.
Judy Yes, I've just put the phone down on them. They're going to erect
another one.
Ross Will it be ready in time for the prize-giving?
Judy They've assured me that it will. My goodness, it better be!
Ross (*smiling*) Thank you, Judy.
Judy Is the weather really going to break, do you think?
Ross It's beginning to look very much like it, I'm afraid. And the forecast
isn't good.

There is a distant roll of thunder and they both turn towards the terrace

Let's hope there isn't a storm. Fay's terrified of lightning — always has
been. (*Pause*) Marian seems to be in a pretty foul mood.
Judy She's been like it ever since she arrived.
Ross Yes. (*Looking at her*) And you've had very little to say for yourself
during the past twenty-four hours, Judy.

Judy makes no comment

Tell me: what do you make of our Danish guest?

Judy He's more or less what I expected.

Ross And what did you expect?

Judy (*vaguely*) Oh — charm, plus ... charm ...

Ross (*moving down to her*) I have a feeling that rather against your better judgement, you've taken quite a liking to him.

Judy You should know me better than that, Ross. Anyway, I'm glad you changed your mind — about not seeing him, I mean. Was it Fay's idea to invite him to the regatta?

Ross (*after a short pause*) No, it was mine. Fay was against it. But I still think it was a good idea. It's lessened the tension, certainly so far as Julian and I are concerned.

Pause

Judy (*puzzled*) Ross, there's something I've been meaning to ask you.

Ross Go ahead.

Judy It's about the Zarabell.

She crosses to the desk, opens the drawer, and takes out the box of Zarabell

Ross (*a faint note of anxiety*) What is it, Judy?

Judy (*opening the box*) It's just that — I thought we had nine phials.

Ross (*firmly*) No. Only eight.

Judy Eight?

Ross Yes.

Judy Are you sure?

Ross Yes. Absolutely. I counted them.

Judy (*her eyes on the box*) That's even more puzzling. There's only seven here.

Ross (*genuinely surprised*) Seven?

Judy Yes.

Ross joins Judy at the desk and examines the contents of the box. Pause

Ross Obviously, we were both mistaken.

Judy Surely, that's very unlikely. But I'll check. There's a list on the file.

Ross thoughtfully replaces the box in the drawer

Alan enters from the terrace. He wears old clothes and his sleeves are rolled up, having just finished working on Ross's boat

Alan (*to Ross*) I decided to do a check-up on *Spring Tide*, Ross — and it's just as well I did. I had to do quite a bit of work on the engine.
Ross Oh, Lord! That sounds ominous.
Alan You should have had the boat serviced weeks ago.
Ross (*shaking his head, regretfully*) Yes, I know. It was very remiss of me.
Alan Well, not to worry. It's OK now.
Ross You're sure?
Alan Yes, I'm quite sure. But I'd like you to take a look at it.

Ross nods and exits on to the terrace

Judy I didn't know you went for that sort of thing.
Alan What sort of thing?

Judy glances down at the spot of oil on his hands and the rag his is holding

(*He smiles*) I've been taking a look at *Toymaker*. It's fantastic! Bill Yorke must be loaded. (*Pause; in a matter-of-fact voice*) Are you going to marry him, Judy?
Judy What makes you think he's asked me?
Alan He's a bit of a damn fool if he hasn't — he's obviously in love with you. (*Pause; with slightly forced brightness*) Well, are you? He's a tolerant, steady sort of chap. If you want my opinion, I think he'd make a super husband.
Judy (*turning*) I don't want your opinion, Alan — and when I do I'll ask for it!
Alan (*pleasantly; completely ignoring the rebuke*) Thank you, Judy.

He stands very near to her and it is a moment or two before she turns away from him

Julian Kane enters from the terrace. He is a distinguished-looking man of indeterminate age. He is wearing well-cut sports clothes as opposed to casual wear. He has a glass of wine in his hand. His voice is pleasant; soft, foreign inflections are noticeable

Julian Oh! Forgive me! I believe I left my lighter in here.

Judy crosses to the table and picks up a gold cigarette lighter

Judy Is this it?
Julian Yes, it is.
Judy I wondered who it belonged to.

Julian joins her, putting his drink down on the table

Julian I never fail to leave it somewhere. Usually in restaurants. One of these days it will disappear for good. (*He takes the lighter from her*) Oh — before I forget. Mr Yorke's asking for you. He's with our host and Dr — Kennedy, is it?
Judy Yes. Sam Kennedy. Thank you.

Judy exits on to the terrace

Pause. Alan's manner is faintly aggressive

Alan Julian ...
Julian (*pleasantly*) Yes, Alan?
Alan Why did you come here this weekend?
Julian I was invited. (*He smiles*) I do get invited out occasionally, you know. If only to play the piano.
Alan Is that why you were invited here? To play the piano?
Julian I hope not. But I fear the worst.
Alan Did Ross invite you?
Julian Yes, he did.
Alan (*darkly*) Because Fay asked him to?
Julian That's quite likely.
Alan Have you told my sister about ... (*he hesitates*)
Julian About what? (*Suddenly*) Oh! About our little transaction? (*He shakes his head*) No. Would you like me to tell her?
Alan Why — why no, of course not!
Julian (*smiling*) Then I won't.

Alan Thank you, Julian.

Julian (*the smile vanishing*) Providing, that is, I receive the money you owe me, by the end of the month.

Alan (*taken aback*) By the end of the month?

Julian At the latest.

Alan But that's impossible! I'm broke. I can't possibly raise eighteen thousand pounds.

Julian You can't?

Alan You know damn well I can't!

Julian (*staring at him*) I would try, Alan. I would try very, very hard if I were in your shoes.

Alan Are you threatening me?

Julian No. But if I don't receive the eighteen thousand — and very soon, my friend — then we move into a different ball game. With very different players, I'm afraid. (*His smile returns*) But not to worry, Alan. You'll raise the money somehow, I'm quite sure you will.

A strained silence

Alan I'll — I'll see what I can do, Julian.

Alan exits on to the terrace

Julian smiles to himself as he crosses to the table. He stands for a moment staring down at his untouched drink. He is about to pick up the glass as ...

Bill enters

Julian Ah! Mr Yorke! I've been wanting to have another word with you. After we'd had our little chat I started thinking. (*He moves towards Bill with a puzzled expression*) Haven't you and I met before, somewhere?

Bill Now, that's curious! *Very* curious!

Julian You had the same feeling?

Bill Yes, I did! Absolutely. In fact, the moment you walked away, I said to myself, I'm jolly sure I've met that chap before somewhere. (*Pause*) But for the life of me, I can't think where it was. Can you?

Julian Could it have been Cape Town?

Bill 'Fraid not. Never been to South Africa. (*Suddenly*) Have you been to Madeira, by any chance?

Julian Only once. I was ten years old at the time.

Bill Oh. (*A dead pause*) You don't happen to know the Pitmans? The Shropshire Pitmans?

Julian I'm afraid I don't. (*He smiles*) I've never been to Shropshire.

Bill Oh, they don't live in Shropshire, they live in Wiltshire. Old Walter Pitman. Fantastic golfer. "Bogey", they used to call him. Superman. (*As an afterthought*) Or was that Roger?

Julian (*amused*) I wouldn't know.

Bill I suppose it's possible we've never actually met, but just seen each other from time to time?

Julian Yes, that's about it, I imagine.

Marian enters from the terrace. She is smoking a cigarette and appears nervous, almost tense

Marian (*to Bill*) It looks as if we're going to be late. Fay's on the committee and she's supposed to be at Mellow House by twelve o'clock.

Julian ignores Marian and, crossing to the window, stands staring out at the sky

Bill Not to worry, we'll make it.

Marian I hope you're right. But what exactly are the arrangements? Who am I going with? No-one's told me anything! I'm completely in the dark!

Bill One's always in the dark at a regatta. You should know that by now, Marian. (*Amused*) Once the arrangements make sense, it's no longer a regatta.

Marian Yes, but what *are* the arrangements?

Bill We're all meeting up for lunch at Mellow House. You're coming with me, Marian. So's Fay.

Marian Yes, well — let's hope *Toymaker*, or whatever you call it, lives up to its reputation.

Bill We shall do our best for you, Marian.

Julian (*returning to Bill; pleasantly*) Why *Toymaker*? I find that a curious name for a boat.

Bill We make toys. My firm, that is.

Julian Ah! I see ...

Bill (*faintly amused*) The first time I saw the boat it was called *Dolly Girl*. It was in Poole Harbour and belonged to a funny little man called Charlie Tube. I made him an offer and after talking it over with his wife ... Dolly, needless to say ——

Marian (*interrupting him; agitated*) It's a very, very long story, Julian!

Both Bill and Julian look at her

Bill (*after a tiny pause; good-naturedly*) I'm afraid Marian's right. It is — rather a long story. Some other time, old boy.

He exits

There is an awkward moment. Julian stares at Marian, distinctly annoyed

Julian Why did you do that? Why did you chase him away like that?

Marian You've been ignoring me, and I've got to talk to you! It's important, Julian.

Julian (*exasperated*) Always you've got to talk to me! When will you realize that nothing you can possible say can be of the slightest importance to me?

Marian (*stung*) Do you think I'm a fool? Do you think I don't know what's going on?

Julian What do you mean?

Marian You know perfectly well what I mean. I'm talking about Fay ...

Julian Leave Fay out of this!

Marian You told me that you were in love with me. You swore nothing, and no-one, would ever come between us ...

Julian I did nothing of the sort!

Marian You did, Julian ...

Julian I was never in love with you. Never! I despise your worst qualities and your best, such as they are, bore me to distraction.

Marian (*stricken*) How can you be so cruel? How can you say such things to me?

Julian I can say them because I feel them! Because I feel them, and they happen to be true! How on earth Laurence managed to live with you all those years, I'll never know.

Marian (*fiercely*) If that's how you felt, why did you make love to me?

Julian (*amused by her question*) Don't you know why? Don't you know why, Marian?

There is a strained silence, then Marian turns away from him and stands for a moment or two staring down at the glass on the table and a nearby ashtray. Then suddenly, viciously, she starts stubbing out her cigarette in the ashtray. After a tense pause, she finally turns and faces Julian again. She is less emotional now, but there is no mistaking the hatred she feels towards him

Marian Do you know what you are, Julian?

Julian No. Tell me.

Marian You're a cruel, ruthless bastard. And mark my words — one of these days someone will have the guts to do something about it!

Julian Well, one thing's for sure, Marian. It won't be you!

Marian is about to retort, then changes her mind and quickly exits

Julian is pleased with himself for having had the last word. He moves down to the table and picks up his glass of wine. He is about to drink when he suddenly feels a sharp pain in his chest. He quickly puts the glass back on the table. It is obvious that he is somewhat alarmed and he stands for a moment, with eyes closed, waiting for the spasm to pass

A long, tense pause

Julian, to his intense relief, slowly recovers and is feeling virtually normal when ...

Judy enters from the terrace carrying a tray bearing several empty glasses, etc. As she moves towards the kitchen she stares at Julian, sensing that something has happened to him

Judy (*hesitantly*) Aren't you feeling well, Mr Kane?

Julian I had a slight dizzy spell a moment ago, but I'm fine now. It happens occasionally.

Judy Can I get you a drink?

Julian No, thank you. As a matter of fact, I've got one. And I think perhaps you'd better get rid of it for me. (*He picks up his drink and takes it across to her, putting it on the tray*) I've been stupid. I really shouldn't drink so early in the day.

Judy give a little nod and goes into the kitchen with the tray. Julian turns towards the terrace

   Fay enters carrying a raincoat

Julian immediately takes hold of her

Fay Darling, don't ... not now ... (*As she breaks away from him*) I'm just about to leave, Julian. (*Anxiously*) Has Ross talked to you?

Julian About us? No, not yet. But he will. Don't worry! Please don't worry, Fay. (*Pause*) I like Ross. I like him very much. But he's not a bit like I expected. Tell me a little more about him, Fay.

Fay (*surprised by the question*) About Ross? What is it you want to know?

Julian Was his father a doctor?

Fay No, he was a lawyer. Ross took a law degree and was about to join the family firm when suddenly, to everyone's astonishment, he decided to go in for medicine. But, in a curious sort of way, they were quite an artistic family. Ross has a younger sister who's a novelist and his mother was an opera singer. Beatrice Marquand. You may have heard of her?

Julian No. But you told me about her.

Fay She was quite well-known in her day.

A short pause

Julian Fay, are you sorry about us? Do you regret what's happened?

Fay No, but I think of Ross a great deal. I can't help it. He depends on me, Julian. Far more than he realizes.

Julian I depend on you too, Fay. (*Pause*) Have you told him about America?

Fay shakes her head

   You're frightened to tell him, is that it?

Fay Yes, I'm frightened.

Julian Then don't tell him! Just pack your things one day and leave.

He stops an immediate protest from Fay

   It would be the kindest thing you could do, Fay. It really would! Why have a scene? You'll both get upset and in the end, you might change your mind.

Fay I shan't ...

Julian But you might! And it's a risk I don't want you to take. Promise me, Fay. Promise me, that's what you'll do? (*He attempts to embrace her*)

Fay (*running towards the terrace*) I must go, Julian! I really must! They'll be waiting for me.

Ross suddenly appears in the window

Fay, coming virtually face to face with Ross, is taken by surprise

Ross Bill's ready to leave, Fay.

Fay Yes. Yes, I'm — just coming, Ross ... (*She glances back at Julian, then looks at Ross, obviously on the verge of saying something*)

Quickly changing her mind, she exits

Ross moves into the room and for a moment the two men face each other

Julian It was kind of you to invite me to the regatta. I haven't been to this sort of thing for ages. I do believe the last time was at Copenhagen, many years ago. (*Pause*) Do you know Copenhagen?

Ross I've been there. Only once. I spent three days at a medical convention. I hardly saw the city and unfortunately I didn't care for my hotel very much.

Julian That can happen. I shall never forget the first time I arrived in London. I hated it. I stayed at a small hotel in Maida Vale called "Bella Vista". I never discovered why.

Ross Do you mean you never discovered why you stayed there, or you never discovered why they called it "Bella Vista"?

Julian Oh, I stayed there for an excellent reason. It was a great deal cheaper than anywhere else.

Ross I see.

Julian When I landed in England I had one suit of clothes, a letter of introduction to a fellow musician, and two hundred and twenty-seven pounds — exactly. So I couldn't very well afford to stay at the Ritz, could I?

Ross No, I suppose not. But you appear to have done well for yourself.

Julian (*smiling*) That was always my intention. (*Pause*) Fay tells me you're very fond of opera.

Ross Yes, I am. Although I don't get to Covent Garden as often as I would like to. (*After a momentary hesitation*) My mother was quite a well-known singer. She sang many times on the Continent.

Julian stares at him, as if trying to recall something

Julian Marquand? (*With apparent astonishment*) Not Beatrice Marquand?
Ross Yes.
Julian How extraordinary! I remember going to the State Opera House in Stockholm to hear your mother sing. She had a beautiful voice.
Ross Stockholm? If I remember rightly that was her last appearance. She died the following year. But fancy your remembering ...
Julian But of course I remember! (*Thoughtfully*) Beatrice Marquand ... She was very tiny, and dark ... and she wore a silver dress. Quite the loveliest dress, I think, I have ever seen. (*With a little laugh*) But she didn't look a bit like an opera singer!
Ross No, I'm afraid she didn't.

Pause

Julian I think you know why I accepted your invitation. Why I wanted to see you.

Ross nods

Then perhaps you'll forgive me if, before anything else, I talk about myself. (*Pause*) All my adult life, I've been the victim of gossip. I've only got to look at a woman and smile, and be pleasant, and act like a normal human being for the media to report that I'm having an affair with her. (*Pause*) Do you remember reading about a girl called Sylvia Cartwright?
Ross I — I seem to recall the name ...
Julian She had an abortion and the poor girl died. There was an article about her in one of the tabloids. It claimed we'd had an affair and I was totally responsible for what happened.
Ross I see. But why are you telling me this?
Julian I'm telling you this because rumours, ugly rumours, still persist and I'd like you to know exactly what happened. Syliva was living with

a friend of mine called Philip Challis. She became pregnant and Philip
was delighted, thrilled, in fact. But, to his astonishment, Sylvia flatly
refused to have the baby. In desperation Philip asked me to talk to her.
I took her out to dinner and did my best, my very best, to persuade her
to have the child. It was no use. She was adamant. Just as I was kissing
her good-night outside the restaurant a photographer took a photograph
of us. When Sylvia died the photograph was published alongside the
nasty little article.

Ross Did you sue the newspaper?

Julian No. I didn't even consult a lawyer. I thought — what the hell!
Whatever happens, people will think what they want to think. (*Pause*)
Now, with hindsight, I'm not sure I made the right decision.

*Ross moves down to the table and stands with his back to Julian. After a
moment, he turns*

Ross Well, I'll say one thing. You've been very honest with me. So far ...

Julian So far? And what does that mean?

Ross It means — I hope you'll continue to be honest with me when we
talk about my wife.

Julian I shall be honest with you whatever we talk about.

Pause

Ross (*his eyes on Julian*) Are you in love with Fay?

Julian Yes, I'm in love with her. More in love than I ever dreamed it was
possible to be in love with anyone.

Ross Then what do you propose to do about it?

Pause

Julian (*a note of sadness in his voice*) Having met you, and seen the two
of you together, in your lovely home, I realize there's only one thing I
can do.

Ross Oh? And what's that?

Julian For some time now I've been debating whether to accept an offer
I've received from America. This morning, I finally reached a decision.
I shall leave for New York — alone, I might add — at the end of this
week.

Ross stares at him, taken by surprise. Never, for one moment, did he expect to hear a statement of this kind

Ross And what will you tell Fay?

Julian I shan't tell her anything. I shall just disappear. I think it's better that way. Better for all of us.

Ross Does Fay know about the American offer?

Julian No. I purposely haven't told her.

A deliberate pause. Ross is trying to reach a decision of some kind

Ross Julian, why do you think I invited you here this weekend?

Julian I don't know. I've wondered about that. You didn't want to see me, did you? Not at first. Then suddenly, you changed your mind. Why? (*Intensely curious*) Why did you do that?

Ross I'd made up my mind to kill you.

Julian is thunderstruck

Julian Kill me?

Ross Yes.

Julian I don't believe this! (*He moves down to Ross*) You can't have been serious?

Ross I was never more serious in my life. (*He takes a phial of Zarabell out of his pocket*) Do you know what this is?

Julian stares at the phial

Julian No. What is it?

Ross It's a phial of Zarabell.

Julian Zarabell?

Ross Yes.

Julian Zarabell Four?

Ross nods

But surely, that's the drug people are worried about. There's been articles in the press about it.

Ross That's right.

Julian (*staring at the phial; puzzled*) Well? Why show me this?

Ross Unless I'm mistaken, some little time ago you had a heart attack. You were in the National Hospital for almost five weeks.

Julian You're not mistaken. But I still fail to see what that's go to do with ... (*he stops; with a sudden realization*) My God! Zarabell!

Ross At some point during the weekend I was going to mix you a drink with Zarabell in it. I knew that, with your medical history, there was every possibility that you'd have another heart attack.

Julian But you must have been crazy to think of doing a thing like that! You must have been out of your mind. Besides which, you just wouldn't have got away with it! Surely you must have realized that?

Ross I wasn't hoping to commit the perfect murder and escape retribution. That was never what I intended. All I wanted was to end your relationship with Fay. (*He puts the phial back in his pocket*) Every single day, every night, I was obsessed by that thought.

An appreciable pause

Julian Well, I'm sorry. Deeply sorry to have caused you such unhappiness. I only hope I've put your mind at rest.

For a moment they take each other in

After this weekend, I promise you, I shall never see Fay again.

He stops a reaction from Ross

I mean that! I really do.

A faintly embarrassed silence

I don't think we've anything else to say to each other, do you?

Ross No, I don't think we have.

There is a brief, awkward moment before Ross exits into the hall

Pause

Julian looks towards the hall. After a pause, he starts laughing. It is obvious that he is laughing at Ross for having been taken in by his story.

He is still amused when he crosses to the open window and stands staring up at the sky. There is a flash of lightning and a long roll of thunder. For several seconds he watches the gathering storm clouds, then finally he turns and moves back into the room. He has reached the centre of the room when he is once again overwhelmed by an agonizing pain. There is a tense pause before Julian is able to grab hold of the table in an attempt to steady himself

He is still holding on to the table when Fay, terrified by the storm, rushes into the room from the terrace

Fay (*alarmed*) What is it, Julian? Are you ill?

Julian looks at her, hardly comprehending what she has said

Julian (*dazed*) What are you doing here? I thought you'd left.
Fay I was frightened of the lightning. We were just about to leave when ——

Julian, in pain, gives a little cry

Julian, you need help!
Julian No, wait! Wait a minute. (*A thought occurs to him*) Why am I feeling like this? There must be a reason. My God! He lied ... he lied to me ... He knew this was going to happen!
Fay (*bewildered*) Lied? Who lied, Julian?
Julian (*terrified; not listening to her*) I need a doctor! Get Dr Kennedy! Please, Fay ...
Fay I'll fetch Ross ...
Julian No! Not Ross. Get Dr Kennedy!

Fay is panic-stricken. She crosses to the window, hesitates because of the lightning, then rushes out on to the terrace. We hear her calling, "Sam!", "Sam, please come here!", "Sam!"

Julian releases his hold on the table. He is, momentarily, feeling a shade better and he makes up his mind to try and reach the comfort of the sofa. He has almost succeeded when a further spasm of pain occurs and he collapses. Pause

Fay returns, quickly followed by Sam. Sam takes in the situation, and goes to Julian's assistance, kneeling down beside him

Julian, in great pain, at once tries to tell Sam something

Sam (*examining him*) Don't talk! Just try and relax ...
Julian (*making a determined effort to speak*) Zarabell ... He must have given me Zarabell ...
Fay What's he saying? What was that about Zarabell?

Sam shakes his head, continuing with his examination

Is he going to be all right?

Sam ignores the question. He is completing his examination when Ross appears in the hall

Ross Fay! Why aren't you with Bill? (*Suddenly becoming aware of Julian as he enters the room*) What is it, Sam? What's happened?
Fay Julian's ill! I think he's had a heart attack.

Ross moves automatically towards the sofa

Ross How bad is he?

Pause. Sam slowly rises

Sam (*shaking his head*) It's too late, Ross. There's nothing we can do.
Fay (*frenzied*) No! Oh, no!

There is a tense, uneasy silence and Ross is suddenly conscious of the fact that Fay is staring at him

The Lights fade

CURTAIN

ACT II

Scene 1

The same. That night

Bill Yorke is alone in the room sitting on the sofa, facing a card table. He is in the final stages of a game of Patience. Pause

The phone rings. Bill merely glances at it, making no attempt to interrupt his game. The phone stops ringing, having been answered in the consulting room. Bill puts down his last card

Alan appears from the terrace

Bill looks up and points to the window

Bill Close the window, Alan, there's a good chap. It's getting quite chilly.

Alan closes the window then moves down to the sofa. His movements are a shade unsteady

Where have you been? We wondered what had happened to you.
Alan I went for a walk. (*A note of irritation in his voice*) Where is everybody? The place is like a morgue. Oh dear! Shouldn't — shouldn't have said that, should I?

Bill looks at him and realizes he has been drinking

Bill I take it, you haven't been walking the whole time?
Alan Very perceptive of you, William. (*He gestures with his hand to indicate the number of drinks*) I've had one or two. Two or three, maybe. (*He steadies himself*) Where's Judy?
Bill (*pointing to the consulting room*) She's dealing with the phone calls.
Alan What phone calls?

Bill Don't be stupid, Alan. The phone's never stopped ringing. It if isn't the regatta people it's the newspapers.

Alan The newspapers? How the devil did they hear about Julian?

Bill I would have thought that was obvious. The police.

Alan Ah! Yes, that figures, I guess. Don't know about you, but I didn't take to that Inspector chap ...

Bill Sanders? He was all right. You can't blame him for being on the ball. Had Ross met him before?

Alan Yes ...

Bill Thought so.

Alan He's by way of being a patient. But who sent for the police in the first place, that's what I'd like to know.

Bill Ross did. He and Sam Kennedy talked things over and they decided it was the best thing to do.

Alan Why, for God's sake?

Bill They were both worried about something Julian said just before he died. Something about Zarabell Four. Also ... (*he hesitates and changes his mind*)

Alan Also what?

Bill (*shaking his head*) It doesn't matter.

Alan Come on, Bill! What were you going to say?

Bill I was going to say ... according to what I've heard ... Fay wasn't too happy either. Apparently there's a doubt in Fay's mind as to what actually happened.

Pause

Alan I see. (*He crosses to the drinks cabinet and proceeds to pour himself a scotch*) And what's your opinion, Bill? Is there a doubt in your mind?

Bill Why, no! Of course there isn't. Julian was taking Zarabell. As a result of which he had a heart attack. Cause and effect. That's how I see it.

Alan How do you know Julian was taking Zarabell?

Bill Dash it all, Alan! Quite apart from what he said to Sam, Julian had a silver pillbox in his pocket. It contained a phial of the stuff.

Alan This is news to me. Who told you about the box?

Bill I'm not sure. Someone did. It might have been Sam.

Alan What's happened to Sam, by the way? I haven't seen him around.

Bill He and his wife left about an hour ago. They're driving up to Scotland early tomorrow morning. I understand their daughter's in a clinic near Perth.

Alan nods, finishes his drink and starts to pour himself another one. Pause

(*Watching Alan*) Don't you think you've had enough to drink, Alan?

Alan That's a leading question. But I must confess I've been expecting it. Still — it's worthy of the most careful consideration. (*He takes a long drink*) The answer's no.

Bill (*smiling*) You'll regret it tomorrow morning.

Alan You overrate me. If I run true to form I shall regret it long before tomorrow morning. (*He moves down to Bill*) However, there's something I want to ask you. Tell me — and be absolutely frank. What was your opinion of the late Mr Kane?

Bill He seemed an amiable sort of person. Bit smooth, perhaps. but I must confess I was surprised to find that he was staying here.

Alan Why?

Bill Just wouldn't have thought Ross would have been friendly with him. Not his sort of chap, I would have said.

Alan And Fay? Was he Fay's sort of chap, do you think?

Bill (*staring at him; irritated by the remark*) Do you know what I'd do, Alan, if I were you?

Alan No, tell me.

Bill I'd take a cold shower, swallow a couple of aspirins, and go to bed for an hour or so.

Alan That sounds to me like remarkably good advice.

Bill It is.

Alan Unfortunately, I'm allergic to good advice. Always have been. Bad advice? Now that's a very different kettle of fish. Just can't resist it. (*He finishes the drink and puts the glass down*)

Ross enters from the hall

Bill Ross, how's Fay? Is she feeling any better?

Ross I think so, Bill. Thank you. I've given her a sedative and she's resting. (*To Alan*) Where's Marian? I haven't caught sight of her since dinner.

Alan I don't know. Don't know where she is. Prob — probably in her room. Sh — she said something about a headache. But that was some time ago. (*Hesitatingly*) Ross, I'm a bit confused at the moment. There's something I don't understand.

Ross I can well imagine there's something you don't understand, Alan.

Alan I know! I've had too much to drink. But I'm not pissed. Believe me, I'm not. Bear with me, Ross.

Ross What is it that's troubling you?

Alan I don't understand why you sent for the police. Bill says it was because of something Julian said. Something about Zarabell ...

Ross Bill's right. But first, there's something I want to tell you both. Something which may, or may not, come out at the inquest. Fay was having an affair with Julian and she wanted me to meet him.

Bill glances at Alan, then looks at Ross

That's why he was here. Why I invited him to the regatta.

Alan (*surprised*) Why *you* invited him?

Ross Yes. The invitation was my idea, not Fay's. (*Pause*) When Julian had the heart attack he cried out for a doctor. I was upstairs at the time and Fay offered to fetch me. Julian stopped her. He wouldn't hear of it. (*He shakes his head; puzzled*) Why he didn't want me to help him, I don't know. We'd just had a long conversation. We'd been quite friendly, in fact ...

Pause

Bill (*quietly*) Go on, Ross.

Ross I told Sam what had happened. I told him the whole story and he was worried. Very worried. Apart from anything else, he felt sure that Julian had been on the verge of telling him something. Something of importance ...

Bill So — in the end you decided to send for the police?

Ross Yes. At the time I felt I had no alternative.

Marian enters from the hall. She is dressed for a journey

Oh, hallo, Marian! How's your headache? Is it any better?

Marian Yes. It's much better, thank goodness. (*She hesitates, ill at ease*) Ross, I'm leaving and I took the liberty of sending for a car. I hope you don't mind?

Ross (*somewhat surprised*) No, of course not.

Marian I suddenly remembered. I can't stay the night. I've got a buyer, a French girl, calling in the boutique first thing tomorrow morning.

Ross That's all right, Marian. You must please yourself. But you're very welcome to stay.

Marian Yes, I know that, darling. (*An uneasy pause*) I'm sorry Fay didn't come down to dinner. I very much wanted to talk to her. I hope she's all right, Ross.

Ross I gave her a sedative. She's probably asleep by now.

Judy enters from the consulting room

Judy (*to Ross*) I've spoken to several of the newspapers, but the editor of the local rag insists on having a word with you. He says he's a friend of yours.

Ross I'll phone him tomorrow. Don't take any more calls. Switch the answering machine on.

Judy nods and moves to leave

Marian (*stopping her*) Judy ...

Judy (*turning*) Yes, Mrs — Marian?

Marian Did *you* see the Inspector whilst he was here?

Judy (*surprised by the question*) Why, yes. (*She glances at the others*) I think we all did. Why do you ask?

Marian Were you questioned about Julian? About what happened?

Judy Yes, of course!

Marian (*hesitant*) Was I mentioned, at all?

Judy You? Why, no.

Ross What is it, Marian? What's worrying you?

Marian I — I was very stupid, I'm afraid. I told the Inspector that I hardly knew Julian. That I'd only met him once before.

Bill And that wasn't true?

Marian No. No, I'm afraid it wasn't.

Ross Why did you do that?

Marian He made me nervous. So nervous I hardly knew what I was saying. If he'd been agressive I could have handled the situation, I could have coped with him. But he wasn't like that. He was pleasant and terribly polite the whole time. (*Worried*) What do you think I ought to do, Ross? Should I see him first thing tomorrow morning and tell him the truth, do you think?

Ross is giving the matter thought

Ross No. No, I don't think so, Marian.

Marian But supposing he finds out I had a row with Julian?

Ross (*taken by surprise*) A row? (*He moves down to her*) You had a row with him?

Marian Well — not exactly a row. He was beastly to me. Really cruel, and I lost my temper.

There is a slight embarrassment on everyone's part before Bill finally speaks

Bill I should forget if I were you. Put it out of your mind.

Judy Yes, of course.

From the drive, the sound of a car horn is heard, announcing the arrival of Marian's car. She looks towards the window

Marian That's my car. I mustn't keep him waiting ...

She dismisses Ross as he moves to join her

It's all right, darling. I can manage. Good-night, Ross. And please — do look after Fay.

She nods to the others and makes a hasty exit. Pause

Judy (*quietly*) She's frightened.

Alan Aren't we all?

Bill And what's that supposed to mean?

Alan It means precisely what you think it means. If the police aren't happy ... if they suspect that Julian was murdered ——

Bill Murdered? Good heavens, what's murder got to do with what happened this morning? Julian had a heart attack brought on by his taking Zarabell Four.

Ross But Bill, supposing Julian wasn't on Zarabell? Supposing someone put the stuff in his drink knowing the effect it would have on him?

Bill (*puzzled*) Well?

Ross Well — wouldn't you call that murder?

Bill Yes, of course I would! But that's not what's happened!

Alan How do you know? Julian had several drinks whilst he was on the terrace. Someone could very easily have put Zarabell in one of them.

Bill That's ridiculous! Absurd! Julian Kane died from a heart attack. There's no doubt about that and at the inquest we've got to get that fact very firmly established. Nothing else.

Ross Yes, but Bill — supposing, just supposing, you knew for a fact that Julian *was* murdered. Would you speak up at the inquest, or remain silent?

Bill (*after a pause*) If Julian was murdered, then one of us must have committed the murder.

Ross Yes, that's obvious. But you still haven't answered the question.

Pause. The three of them are staring at Bill

Bill (*slowly; thoughtfully*) It's always been a conviction of mine, ever since I was a boy, that under exceptional circumstances — exceptional, mark you! — a person would be justified in taking the law into their own hands. Does that answer your question?

Ross Yes. Yes, I suppose it does.

Bill Good! (*He smiles at them*) Now, having been to confession, if you don't mind, I'll say good-night.

Ross Good-night, Bill.

Alan Good-night.

Bill Judy ...

Judy (*staring at Bill; a shade puzzled*) Good-night.

Bill exits

Alan (*looking at Ross*) In view of what's been said, I think there's something you should know, Ross.

Ross And what's that?

Alan If it *was* murder, then Marian wasn't the only one with a motive.

Ross (*quietly*) I'm aware of that.

Alan (*shaking his head*) I'm not referring to you, if that's what you're thinking.

Ross Then who are you referring to?

Alan Myself. Good-night, Ross. Good-night, Judy ...

He exits

Ross (*at a loss*) What on earth was all that about? What possible motive could Alan have had?

Judy He borrowed eighteen thousand pounds from Julian.

Ross (*amazed*) Alan did? I didn't know that!

Judy Julian suddenly became difficult and threatened to speak to Fay about the loan.

Ross Who told you this?

Judy Alan.

Ross I see. (*A thoughtful pause*) Judy, I've been meaning to ask you. Did you check the Zarabell list?

Judy Yes — and I was right. We had nine phials to start with.

Ross And now there's only seven?

Judy Yes.

Pause

Ross What, in your opinion, happened to the other two?

Pause

Judy I don't know.

Ross Oh, come on, Judy! You must have some idea.

There is a brief silence

Judy ...

Judy I think that you took one of the phials with the intention of giving it to Julian, but at the last moment, for some reason or other, you changed your mind.

Ross And the other one?

Judy I can only assume that was taken by ... someone else ...

Ross By someone else?

Judy (*not looking at him*) Yes.

Ross (*in a noncommittal tone of voice*) You must be right, of course. (*He hesitates, then*) Good-night, my dear.

Judy Good-night, Ross.

Ross exits

Judy, deep in thought, glances at her watch then moves about the room, tidying the sofa and rearranging the various articles on the table. She is

*returning to the consulting room when the front doorbell rings. Pause. The
doorbell rings again*

    Judy quickly crosses the room and exits into the hall

After a moment we hear the opening of a door

Sanders (*off*) I'm sorry to disturb you, Miss Hilton. But may I come in?

Pause

    *Judy enters with Chief Inspector Norman Sanders. Sanders is a well-
    educated man in his late thirties. There are times when he makes his
    professional charm go a very long way*

Judy I'll tell Dr Marquand you're here.
Sanders (*stopping her*) No, no, please! Don't disturb the good doctor. It's
    you I wanted to see.
Judy Me?
Sanders Yes. I'd rather like to have another word with you, Miss Hilton,
    before the inquest. (*He smiles*) I hope you don't mind?
Judy (*coldly*) No, I don't mind. Sit down, Inspector.
Sanders Thank you. (*He sits in one of the armchairs; in a friendly tone*)
    How is Mrs Marquand? Is she feeling any better?
Judy I think so. But I haven't seen a great deal of her since you left. The
    doctor gave her a sedative and insisted she rest.
Sanders Very wise. She was certainly very upset when I saw her. But
    then, it was to be expected. One minute she was terrified of the storm and
    the very next minute Mr Kane was having a heart attack. Most distress-
    ing for her.
Judy Do you think we might come to the point, Inspector? Why are you
    here?
Sanders I'd just like to ask you a few questions, Miss Hilton.
Judy Go ahead. But why couldn't you have asked me these questions this
    morning? You had the opportunity.
Sanders I did indeed. But it so happens, when I returned to my office my
    secretary told me something which, to say the least, made me curious.

Pause

Judy Well? Aren't you going to tell me what it was that aroused your curiosity?

Sanders Yes, I am. But first, tell me: had you met Mr Kane prior to this weekend?

Judy No, I hadn't. Well — that's not strictly true. I was introduced to him, very briefly, at a party. It was a long time ago.

Sanders Did you remind him of that fact?

Judy No, I didn't.

Sanders Why not?

Judy I felt sure he wouldn't remember me and I didn't wish to embarrass him. Or myself either, for that matter.

Sanders Why was he invited to spend the weekend here, do you know?

Judy There's always people staying here when the regatta's taking place.

Sanders I see. (*A tiny pause*) My secretary — Betty Wilder — is a very attractive girl and about a year ago she appeared in a television documentary, *Women in Uniform*. After the transmission there was a party and Julian Kane suddenly appeared. Apparently he'd been rehearsing in one of the other studios. He was introduced to Betty and he ...

Judy Made a pass at her?

Sanders Yes. He made a pass at her. In fact, he asked her to have dinner with him and they fixed a date for the following week.

Judy And did she have dinner with him?

Sanders No. The next day she bumped into an old friend and, typical of Betty, she started shooting a line about her dinner date. It transpired her friend knew Kane. She said he was a complete womanizer and for the likes of Betty it was simply an invitation to join the bed and breakfast brigade.

Judy I see. And that's all. (*With a note of derision*) That little story made you curious?

Sanders That and the fact that Betty saw Kane one day last week. He was with a well-dressed woman and they were getting out of a taxi. Betty recognized the woman. It was Mrs Marquand. (*Pause*) In other words, Miss Hilton, am I mistaken? Are we both mistaken in fact? Was Julian Kane a friend of *Mrs* Marquand's?

Judy Look, Inspector! Suppose you stop beating about the bush.

Sanders Am I beating about the bush?

Judy Yes, you are. You're asking me in a roundabout way whether Fay — Mrs Marquand — was having an affair with Julian Kane.

Sanders And was she?

Judy Not to my knowledge.

Sanders (*pleasantly*) Thank you. That's really all I wanted to know. (*He rises*)

Judy It seems to me, Inspector, your imagination's running away with you.

Sanders It's possible. It does from time to time.

Judy Well — may I make a suggestion?

Sanders Please do.

Judy Instead of asking me questions, I would suggest you ask yourself one.

Sanders Which particular question have you in mind?

Judy If Mrs Marquand were having an affair with Kane would the doctor have invited him down here for the weekend?

Sanders Ah! Now that *is* an interesting question, I admit. And to be truthful, it's one I've been asking myself all evening. (*Pleasantly*) And it rather looks as if I shall have to go on asking myself it. Miss Hilton, I won't take up any more of your time. You've been most helpful.

Judy (*a shade puzzled*) I'm glad you think so.

Sanders exits, followed by Judy

After a moment Judy re-enters from the hall. She stands for a little while turning over in her mind the conversation she has had with the Inspector, before finally going into the consulting room

Long pause

Alan enters from the hall. He now appears to be reasonably sober, but he is obviously dejected and overwrought. He stands staring at the room with unseeing eyes before making his way down to the desk

As he sits at the desk he appears unmistakably tense, as if on the verge of making a momentous decision. Finally, he selects a sheet of notepaper and begins to write a note. When the note is finished he folds it and places it in a noticeable position on top of the desk. Having done this he takes a gun out of his pocket

There is a long pause, during which Alan sits staring at the gun. Finally, he opens his mouth and slowly raises the barrel of the gun to his face

At this moment Judy comes out of the consulting room and immediately sees what is happening

Judy (*almost a scream*) Alan!

Alan turns, completely taken by surprise

Alan (*desperately*) Go away! Go away, Judy!

Judy rushes across to the desk and grabs hold of his arm

Judy What in God's name do you think you're doing?
Alan (*vehemently*) Go away! Leave me alone!
Judy Don't be a bloody fool, Alan! (*She snatches the gun out of his hand and in desperation throws it across the room*)

Alan, emotionally disturbed, buries his head in his hands. An uncertain pause. Judy notices the note he has written. She picks it up and is reading the note when Alan slowly rises

Alan (*as Judy finally takes her eyes off the note*) Well — now you know!
Judy Yes Alan — now I know.
Alan You didn't think I'd have the guts to kill him, did you, Judy? Well, I did — and I'm not sorry!
Judy Aren't you, Alan? (*A moment*) Why did you kill Julian? Tell me! I'm quite sure it wasn't because of the money owed him.
Alan You're too sure of a great many things. Yourself included.
Judy (*taken aback, but not offended*) Oh. Oh, indeed?
Alan (*facing her*) I'm sorry, but I've been wanting to tell you that for a very long time.
Judy Then why didn't you?
Alan Because I've never had the opportunity.
Judy You should have made the opportunity, Alan.

They look at one another steadily, then suddenly, and quite without warning, he takes her into his arms and kisses her. After a moment Judy responds to his kiss

After a long pause, Alan releases her

(*Shaking her head*) You didn't kill Julian!

Alan No! But I intended to. That's why I stole the Zarabell. (*He produces a phial of Zarabell*)

Judy You thought Ross was responsible for Julian's death and you decided to take the blame?

Alan nods

You're a fool, Alan. But albeit, a courageous one. Now — let me put your mind at rest. You're wrong about Ross!

Alan Wrong?

Judy Yes. Totally wrong.

Alan Then who did kill Julian?

Judy makes no comment. She stares at Alan and slowly tears up the note

Black-out

SCENE 2

The same. Several days later. Afternoon

Sam is seated in one of the armchairs listening to Ross, who is reclining on the sofa. Sam's case is by the side of the chair

Ross I'm glad you were impressed by the clinic, Sam. But I felt sure you would be. They've done a first-rate job, especially when you consider what they were up against. But tell me: what did you make of Dr Lestrade?

Sam To be perfectly honest, when my wife and I first met him we didn't know what on earth to make of the chap.

Ross smiles

But later, when we saw him with some of the young people we realized what a terrific job he was doing. And Liz has obviously taken to him, thank goodness.

Ross How was Liz? How did she look?

Sam Much the same. Although curiously enough, we both felt there'd been a slight improvement in her.

Ross In what way?

Sam She still has very little to say for herself. But she listens now, listens to what other people are saying. Which could be a change for the better, in my opinion.

Ross I agree. (*Pause*) You said, on the phone, there was something else you wanted to talk about.

Sam Yes, I did. Believe it or not, just before we left for Scotland, the Inspector telephoned me.

Ross Sanders?

Sam (*nodding*) He asked me a whole lot of questions. Questions I'd already answered. Was I sure Julian had mentioned Zarabell? Was I convinced that he'd been trying to say something to me just before he died?

Ross I'm not surprised to hear this, Sam.

Sam No?

Ross No. He's calling on me sometime this afternoon. I don't know why. And he's already had another session with Judy. (*He rises*) Incidentally, I don't know whether Sanders mentioned it. The inquest is scheduled for Monday afternoon.

Sam Yes. He told me. (*He rises*) It would be a Monday. Always a hectic day for me. Still there's nothing I can do about it. (*A slight hesitation*) What do you think will happen?

Ross I'm not sure. It's difficult to say.

Pause

Sam Did you make a mistake in sending for the police, do you think?

Ross I don't think I had any choice, Sam. There was obviously a doubt in your mind as to what happened — and Fay wasn't all that happy.

Sam It was what Julian said — or rather, what he was trying to say — that worried me.

Ross Yes, I know. I realize that.

Fay enters. She is surprised to see Sam

Fay Why, hallo, Sam!

Sam Fay, my dear!

Fay (*as he greets her*) How are you? Did you go to Scotland? Did you see Liz?

Sam Yes, we did. We only got back this morning.

Fay How is she?

Sam She's — well, let's just say we're keeping our fingers crossed. We're worried about the drug situation, of course. Who wouldn't be? But thanks to Ross, she's in very good hands.

Fay glances at Ross

Ross It'll take some time, Sam, but she'll be all right. I've told Dr Lestrade to keep you posted.

Sam Thank you, Ross. We're terribly grateful. We really are. (*Moving towards the hall; to Fay*) We don't know what we'd have done without him.

Ross Nonsense!

Sam Good-bye, Fay. Take care of yourself.

Fay You too, Sam.

Sam exits, followed by Ross

Fay is alone for a little while and undecided what to do. She is on the verge of returning to the hall when ...

Ross re-enters. Pause

(*Nervously making conversation*) I've had my sister on the phone. She's not well ...

Ross Oh, I'm sorry.

Fay It's nothing serious, but I thought I'd stay with her for a few days.

Ross nods

She's talking of going on a cruise at the end of the month and she's asked me to go with her.

Ross Are you going?

Fay I don't know. I haven't decided.

Ross The last time you went on a cruise you said never again.

Fay Yes, I know.

Ross You said it more than once.

Fay Did I?

Ross (*smiling*) You wanted me to sue the travel agent. I should bear that in mind, if I were you.

Pause

Fay Where's Judy?
Ross I made her take the day off. She's spending it with Alan.
Fay Oh.
Ross You know what's happened to those two, I imagine?
Fay Yes. Judy told me.
Ross Well — let's hope it works out for them.

Pause. They are staring at each other

Ross What is it, Fay?
Fay I'm sorry, Ross, but — there's something I've got to know. Something I've got to ask you ...
Ross Was I responsible for Julian's heart attack?

Fay nods

Did I, in fact, kill him?
Fay Did you?
Ross No. But I intended to. I'd made up my mind to kill him. That's why I insisted he come to the regatta. And then suddenly, thank God — I realized that not only was I going to destroy Julian, but myself as well. (*Pause*) Also, to be honest with you, Fay, he'd won me over. The more I listened to Julian, the more I liked the man. Finally, when he told me that he was going to America ... (*he stops*) But of course, you knew nothing about that ——
Fay (*taken aback*) America? He told you about America?
Ross Yes.
Fay What did he tell you?

Something in her voice makes him hesitate

Ross He told me that having been here over the weekend, having seen the two of us together, he'd made up his mind to leave you. He said he's accepted an offer from the States and would be leaving for New York at the end of the week.

Fay (*stunned*) He told you that?
Ross Yes.

Fay slowly turns away from him. Pause

(*Puzzled*) What is it, Fay? (*Pause*) What is it?

Fay's answer is a hardly perceptible shake of the head. There is a tense pause, which is finally broken by the ringing of the doorbell

Ross looks towards the hall

Ross That could be the Inspector ...
Fay (*turning; surprised*) Are you expecting him?
Ross Yes. He telephoned this morning and said he'd like to see me.
Fay (*a shade apprehensive*) What does he want, do you know?
Ross No, I don't. Except that he's had another talk to Judy and he
    questioned Sam again. (*He indicates the consulting room*) I think maybe
    you'd better leave us, Fay. I'll join you later.

   *Fay hesitates, then with a little nod, exits into the consulting room. Ross
   exits into the hall. Pause*

   Voices are heard, then Ross re-enters with Sanders

Sanders It's good of you to see me, sir. I shall only keep you a few
    minutes.
Ross (*indicating one of the armchairs*) Sit down, Inspector.

Sanders sits in one of the armchairs

Sanders I expect Miss Hilton told you. Since we last met I've been
    making inquiries about Mr Kane.
Ross (*deliberately vague*) I believe she mentioned something of the sort.
Sanders Did she tell you what my secretary said about him?
Ross No.
Sanders My secretary — a very attractive girl, by the way — knew Kane.
    That is, she'd met him. She described him, in no uncertain terms, as a
    notorious womanizer.

Ross Did she? Did she, indeed?

Sanders Was that your opinion of him, sir?

Ross No. But then, I'm not a woman, Inspector.

Sanders Mr Kane died from a heart attack which was brought on by his taking a dose of Zarabell. I think we're agreed on that?

Ross Yes, I think we are, Inspector.

Sanders Did you prescribe the medication, doctor?

Ross Certainly not. Mr Kane wasn't even a patient of mine. I had no idea he was on Zarabell.

Sanders No idea? Surely, you must have known, sir. He was a friend of yours.

Ross (*pleasantly*) You don't appear to be as well-informed as usual, Inspector. Mr Kane was not a friend of mine.

Sanders (*surprised*) No, sir?

Ross No. My wife and I met him two or three times. Certainly no more.

Sanders And on the strength of that you invited him to spend the weekend with you?

Ross We invited him to the regatta. The regatta needed publicity and Kane was by way of being a celebrity.

Sanders Ah! I see, sir. I understand. (*He rises*) So — correct me if I'm mistaken. What you're saying is you knew very little about Mr Kane?

Ross That's right.

Sanders And, in any case, his private life was no concern of yours.

Ross Exactly!

Sanders faces Ross and plays his ace

Sanders Then why did you take the trouble to investigate him?

Ross (*completely taken aback*) Investigate him?

Sanders Yes, sir.

Ross (*hesitating*) I'm — not sure I know what you mean.

Sanders I think you do, doctor. (*A significant pause*) Shall I tell you what I think happened, sir?

Ross If you feel you must.

Sanders It's my opinion your wife struck up a friendship with Kane and you were worried about it. So worried, in fact, that you asked a Private Inquiry agent, Ashley Richardson, to delve into Mr Kane's background and find out everything he possibly could about him. (*Pause*) Well, sir?

Ross (*with a note of anxiety, almost anger*) Well, what?

Sanders Am I right?

Ross is trying desperately hard to think of a satisfactory explanation when Fay suddenly enters from the consulting room

Fay Perhaps you'd allow me to answer your question, Inspector?

Sanders turns, taken by surprise

Sanders By all means, Mrs Marquand, since your husband would appear to have difficulty in doing so.

Fay looks at Ross

Fay I can't imagine why. (*She moves to Sanders*) You're quite right. My husband did "investigate" Mr Kane, as you call it. And for a very good reason.
Sanders Oh? And what was that?
Fay I asked him to.
Sanders *You* asked him to?
Fay Yes.
Sanders Why would you do that?

A brief pause

Fay I'll be frank with you, Inspector. What you've just said to my husband is true. But only up to a point. I did like Julian Kane. I liked him very much, and I persuaded Ross to invite him down here for the weekend. Unfortunately, after we'd issued the invitation I started hearing stories about him, stories which, quite frankly, astounded me.
Sanders Who told you these stories?
Fay I'd rather not say.
Sanders Mrs Palmer?
Fay I'd rather not say. (*Pause*) The stories just didn't make sense. Not to me, at any rate. Nevertheless — (*she hesitates*) I was curious. In the end, I confided in my husband ...

Sanders glances at Ross

... and I asked him to try and find out if there were any truth in the rumours. (*She shakes her head*) He didn't wish to do that. He said the stories were no concern of ours. Finally, however ...

Sanders You persuaded him to consult Ashley Richardson?
Fay Yes, I did! And I wish now I hadn't.

Sanders gazes at Fay steadily for some time without speaking. finally he gives a non-committal shake of the head and turns away from her

Sanders Thank you for your help, Mrs Marquand. (*He crosses towards the hall*) Doctor ...

Ross moves to join him

Please don't trouble, sir. I can see myself out.

He exits

There is a long pause. Fay and Ross stand in still silence, looking at each other. Fay breaks the mood

Fay He suspected you.
Ross (*softly*) Yes, I know. (*Pause*) Thank you, Fay.

The Lights quickly fade

SCENE 3

The same. Late Monday afternoon

Ross is on the phone. Sam is standing near him, obviously interested in the conversation which is taking place

Ross (*into the phone*) What time would that be? ... (*Surprised*) As early as that? ... Had Bill any other appointments, do you know? ... The inquest was at three, we've just this minute got back. ... Yes, that's a good idea! Please do that. ...(*He hangs up and turns to Sam*) Bill left the office just after one o'clock.
Sam One o'clock? Then why wasn't he at the inquest? He allowed himself plenty of time.
Ross His secretary's just as puzzled as we are. She's making some inquiries.

Sam (*glancing at his watch*) Ross, I must move! I've got a surgery this evening and more than likely a couple of house calls. (*He moves towards the hall*) I'm glad things turned out the way they did.

Ross It's a relief, I must say. And I'm more than grateful to you, Sam. You've been a tremendous help. (*As Sam shakes his head*) Oh, yes! It was you that persuaded Dr Thornton to give evidence. The old boy impressed the coroner and from that moment onwards the Inspector changed his tune. I could see it happening.

Sam It was certainly a stroke of luck, my bumping into Thornton that morning. I hadn't seen him for ages.

As Sam and Ross reach the hall, a somewhat jaded-looking Bill enters

Ross Bill!

Bill What a day! What a ghastly day! I'm sorry I missed the inquest, Ross. I just couldn't help it ...

Ross What happened?

Bill A crazy girl crashed into my car on the M-twenty-five.

Ross Good heavens!

Sam Was anyone hurt?

Bill No — fortunately. But her car was a write-off and the only way I could stop a bout of hysteria was to drive her home. Home being Stoke D'Abernon, I might add!

Ross My dear fellow, you need a drink.

Bill No! Not now, Ross. (*Desperate for news*) What happened this afternoon? Tell me, how did the inquest go?

Sam It went well. Extremely well, in fact. They accepted the fact that Julian had been taking Zarabell against doctor's orders. But Ross will tell you all about it. (*To Ross*) We'll be in touch. I'll phone you during the week.

Sam exits

Bill (*looking at Ross*) This is good news.

Ross Yes. Very.

Bill Were you surprised by the verdict, if that's the right word?

Ross No, not entirely. One day last week Sam bumped into a Dr Thornton. Thornton had looked after Julian from time to time and he told the coroner that Julian had been a most difficult patient. He said he was not a bit surprised that Julian had been taking Zarabell. Julian always knew better, was how Thornton put it.

Bill And that convinced the coroner?

Ross That, plus the fact that the police found a phial of Zarabell on Julian. It was in a silver pillbox which he carried around with him.

Bill Who gave evidence, apart from yourself?

Ross Dr Thornton, Fay, Judy and Inspector Sanders. The coroner didn't call either Alan or Marian. Which was fortunate for Marian because she wasn't there.

Bill Why was that?

Ross I believe she's away. Fay telephoned the boutique this morning and a girl said something about her being in Paris. (*He smiles*) It's what's known as keeping a low profile. (*Pause*) Judy was splendid. She really was. No waffle, no nonsense, never lost for a word. She impressed the coroner no end — and everyone else for that matter.

Bill I can believe that. (*After a slight hesitation*) I don't know if Judy told you, Ross. I asked her to marry me. She turned me down.

Ross No, she didn't tell me. I'm sorry, Bill.

Bill Didn't think she'd accept me, but it was worth a try. (*A slight hesitation, looking at Ross*) I understand Alan's the lucky man?

Ross Yes. And knowing Alan, I've got mixed feelings. I wish I hadn't.

Bill (*shaking his head*) Knowing Judy, it'll work. She's a super person and she knows what she's letting herself in for.

An appreciable pause

What do you think happened, Ross?

Ross I've told you what happened.

Bill I don't mean at the inquest. I mean — what do you think happened to Julian?

Ross I agree with Dr Thornton and the coroner. I think he was stupid about his health.

Bill He ignored what the doctor told him and took Zarabell?

Ross (*a shade hesitant*) Yes.

Bill But why would he do that?

Ross Zarabell has advantages as well as disadvantages. Apart from being a pain reliever it makes the patient feel good. Very good. For a time, at any rate.

Bill (*not convinced*) I see.

Pause

Ross You don't go along with that?

Bill No, I'm afraid I don't.

Ross Well — what's your opinion? What do you think happened?

Pause

Bill I think Julian was murdered.

Ross Murdered? That's not what you said the night of the regatta.

Bill I know. At that point I didn't want the question of murder discussed, or even mentioned.

Ross Why not?

Pause

Why not, Bill?

Bill Because it so happens I gave Julian a drink that morning.

Ross (*taken aback*) You did?

Bill It was shortly after I arrived. Drinks were being offered all round and I was just about to help myself to one when I spotted Julian. He was standing on his own, near the river, taking a good look at *Toymaker*. It was then that I decided to take two drinks. One for me and one for Julian.

Ross (*puzzled*) Well?

Bill Supposing — just supposing — I'd had a phial of Zarabell in my pocket and I'd previously made up my mind to kill Julian. It would have been quite simple for me, wouldn't it? I could have poured the Zarabell into his drink without arousing the slightest suspicion.

Ross But don't be ridiculous! Why would you want to do that? And where would you get the Zarabell from, anyway?

Bill Oh, come on, Ross! You can get practically anything if you're prepared to pay for it. You don't even need a prescription in some countries.

Ross But you didn't know Julian! You'd never met him until that weekend.

Bill Oh, yes! Yes, I had. But he didn't remember me.

Ross Where did you meet him?

Bill Curiously enough, I met him briefly, very briefly, at an inquest. (*Pause*) I've always been fond of Fay, you know. Fond of you too, Ross.

(*Resentfully, yet with the suggestion of a smile*) I shouldn't have like it very much if, after all these years, Julian had taken Fay away from you.

Ross And you think he'd have succeeded in doing that?

Bill Yes, I do.

Ross You appear to know a great deal about Julian, considering you only met him once. You say it was at an inquest?

Bill Yes. Do you remember a girl called Norma Craig?

A brief pause

Ross Wasn't there a portrait of her one year, in the Royal Academy?

Bill Yes, there was. It was called *The Golden Girl* and it created quite a stir. Shortly after the portrait appeared I met Norma at the London Boat Show. Like me she was mad on boats. We fell in love and became engaged. About a month before we were due to get married she went skiing in Switzerland. Someone, a friend I imagine, introduced her to Julian. (*Pause*) She wrote me a letter, breaking off the engagement. It was a very nice letter, but I remember thinking at the time, it didn't sound very much like Norma. (*Pause*) The inevitable happened, of course. He walked out on her. (*Pause*) She was just twenty-one when she committed suicide.

Ross (*aghast*) What are you saying? What are you telling me? That you killed Julian?

Bill I'm telling you that years ago I wanted to kill him. I actually made up my mind to do so. But at that particular moment in time I just hadn't the courage to go through with it.

Ross And last weekend you had the courage. Is that it?

Bill No. People like me never change, Ross.

Ross (*quietly; staring at him*) Never?

Bill (*smiling*) Well — hardly ever ...

The Lights quickly fade

SCENE 4

Three days later. A sunny afternoon. The windows are open

Sanders enters from the consulting room, followed by Ross. Sanders is carrying his overcoat and hat

Sanders It was good of you to see me, doctor. I appreciate it.

Ross (*helping him on with his coat*) It's the old trouble, I'm afraid. Now remember what I've told you. Take the pills until the end of the month. And try not to miss one.

Sanders (*apprehensively*) I do hate taking things.

Ross I know you do. But this is important.

Sanders (*none too happy*) Four pills a day?

Ross That's right.

Sanders It seems an awful lot.

Ross makes no comment

What about alcohol?

Ross That's OK. In moderation.

Sanders A glass of non-alcoholic beer on a festive occasion? Is that it?

Ross (*smiling*) Just try and keep off spirits. (*As they move towards the hall*) If you get worried or have a problem, don't hesitate to give me a ring. Meanwhile, I'll drop your GP a note.

They exit into the hall. Pause

Sanders (*off; surprised*) Oh! Why, Mrs Palmer! Good-afternoon ...

Marian (*off*) Good-afternoon, Inspector. (*Nervously*) May I see you, Ross?

Ross (*off*) Yes, of course, Marian. Go along in ...

Marian enters. She is not her usual self. Her face is drawn and she looks distinctly tired. She opens her handbag, looks at herself in a mirror and touches her hair. She is returning the mirror to her handbag when ...

Ross enters

I'm sorry, Marian. Fay isn't here, I'm afraid.

Marian (*tensely*) Yes, I know.

Ross What have you been doing with yourself recently? We've been trying to get in touch with you.

Marian (*hesitantly; not very convincing*) I've been busy one way and another. The Paris dress shows are on at the moment ... I've been over there ...

Ross Oh! (*Pause*) How was Paris?

Marian Expensive. But I was only there forty-eight hours.

Ross (*making conversation*) It's years since I was in Paris. They tell me it's changed a great deal. Especially the Champs-Elysées.

Marian Yes. That's not what it was, I'm afraid. (*An awkward pause*) Ross, I'm glad Fay isn't here because it's you I wanted to talk to.

Ross (*curious*) Well — sit down, Marian.

Marian sits in one of the armchairs

   Can I get you anything? Some coffee, perhaps?

Marian No. No, thank you, Ross. (*An awkward pause*) I haven't been feeling well lately ...

Ross I'm sorry.

Marian And I'm hoping you might be able to help me, or tell me ... what I should do ...

He studies her for a moment

Ross What seems to be the trouble?

Marian is on the verge of saying something, then changes her mind

   What do you think is the matter with you?

No response

   Are you taking anything?

Marian (*with a shrug*) I've had the odd valium.

Ross (*smiling*) What do you mean, "the odd valium"? How many? When?

Marian I've been taking them for the past ... Oh, I don't know ... ever since the regatta.

Ross How many? (*Pause*) One a day? Two a day? (*Pause*) Three, perhaps?

Marian (*vaguely*) Three a day, maybe. Four some days.

Ross Who gave you the prescription? I certainly didn't.

Marian I have a doctor friend. I — I see him from time to time. He's very helpful.

Ross Have you seen him recently?

Marian No.

Ross Why not?

Marian There are things I couldn't tell him. Things I daren't tell anyone. Except you, Ross.

Ross (*staring at her, mystified*) What sort of things? What are you referring to?

Marian I've got something on my mind the whole time. Something I can't forget, however hard I try. I wake up in the middle of the night wishing to God there was someone I could confide in.

Ross Maybe you should see a psychiatrist. There's a colleague of mine in Harley Street ——

Marian (*tensely; stopping him*) No! No, Ross! You're the only one. The only one that can really understand what I'm going through.

Ross Why me, Marian? I know you're a friend of Fay's, you always have been. But you and I have never been close. Have we, my dear?

Marian (*with a suggestion of panic*) Does that mean you won't help me?

Ross Of course I'll help you! I'll help you in any way I can. (*He draws nearer to her*) But first, relax for a moment and let me feel your pulse. (*He stands by her chair and quietly takes her pulse. A long pause. Finally, releasing her wrist*) That's all right. Quite all right. (*In a friendly tone*) Now, what is it, Marian? What is it that's troubling you?

Marian It's Julian ...

Ross Julian?

Marian I was crazy about him. Mad about him. He gave me to understand that once I'd divorced Laurence we'd be married. Then one day a friend told me that he hadn't the slightest intention of marrying me. That the only reason he'd made love to me was because my husband paid him to. I didn't believe the story. I refused to believe it! But when he started seeing Fay and ignoring my phone calls I realized it was true ...

Pause

Ross Go on, Marian.

Marian That morning, Ross ... when we were on the terrace ... I suddenly saw Bill walk across to Julian and offer him a drink. Julian was standing by the river looking at *Toymaker*. I made a point of joining them and a few minutes later, when Bill moved away, I deliberately bumped into Julian, knocking the glass out of his hand.

Ross Why on earth did you do that?

Marian Why?
Ross Yes.
Marian (*quietly*) Don't you know why?
Ross No, I don't.

Pause

Marian It enabled me to get Julian another drink.
Ross Another drink? (*A tiny pause; puzzled*) I'm sorry, Marian. What is it you're trying to tell me?

A tense pause. Marian rises

Marian I killed Julian. It was because of me that he had the heart attack ...
Ross (*incredulously*) You?
Marian Yes. I put the Zarabell in his drink ... (*Miserably; stumbling*) Later, when I realized what I'd done, I became frightened and cornered Julian. Had he been nice to me I'd have told him about the Zarabell. There was still time. At that point he hadn't touched his drink. It was still over there, on the table. (*From now on her manner becomes increasingly distracted*) But he wasn't nice! He was cruel and vindictive and he went out of his way to hurt me! For a time I had no regrets, then one day it suddenly dawned on me that I'd done a terrible thing. That I'd actually killed someone! Ever since then, no matter where I am, or what I'm doing, I keep thinking of Julian and what happened that morning.

She is visibly shaken and Ross gently takes hold of her. Pause

Ross (*quietly*) You didn't kill Julian. You didn't kill anyone, Marian.
Marian But I did, Ross!
Ross You think you did, and you've good reason for thinking so. (*He shakes his head*) But that's not what happened. Julian wasn't feeling well before he had the fatal heart attack. Judy came into the room and commented on the fact. The glass of wine — the drink you gave him — was untouched. Judy took it away, disposed of the wine, and put the glass in the dishwasher.
Marian (*staring at him; stunned*) I don't believe this, Ross! It isn't true! You're just being kind to me. You're only saying this because you think that I might ——

Ross (*stopping her; with quiet authority*) I've told you the truth. I've told you exactly what happened. (*He releases his hold on her*) If you don't believe me I suggest you talk to the Inspector. He questioned Judy about the drink. Or better still, talk to Judy. She'll confirm what I've told you.

Marian now realizes that he has told her the truth and she suddenly experiences an enormous sense of relief

Marian My God, Ross, you've no idea what this means to me! You've no idea what I've been through ...

Ross Yes, well — don't think about it any longer. Forget the incident. Put it out of your mind. Promise me you'll do that, Marian.

Marian, emotionally grateful, gives a little nod

Promise?

Marian Yes, I promise. (*She smiles at him now with intense relief. She takes out her mirror again, happily studying herself, this time with obvious satisfaction*)

Ross I'll get Fay to phone you, Marian.

Marian Yes, please do. I shall be at the boutique all day tomorrow.

The telephone rings

Ross Excuse me. (*He answers the phone*) Hallo? ... Oh! Er — could you hold on a moment, I've got someone with me. (*He sets the phone down and looks at Marian, a direct hint that she should leave*)

Marian takes the hint and quickly puts her mirror away. She crosses to Ross, puts her arms around him and kisses him

Marian I won't keep you any longer, darling! I can't begin to tell you how grateful I am! Give Fay my love when you see her.

She quickly exits

Ross looks into the hall, making absolutely sure she has left. Finally he returns and picks up the phone

(*Into the phone*) Sorry, Fay. ... Marian was here. ... Yes, Marian! ... She surfaced about ten minutes ago. ... I didn't think it was a good idea, Fay. ... She's been very worried and I didn't want her to go into details on the phone. I'll tell you all about it when I see you. ... How's your sister? ... Oh, good! I'm glad to hear that. ... Does that mean you'll be coming home tomorrow? ... I see. ... Well — I'll be here, if you need me. Give my love to Diana. (*He hangs up*)

Bill suddenly appears at the open window

Bill May I come in?

Ross (*turning; taken by surprise*) Why, hallo, Bill! Yes, of course.

Bill (*stepping into the room*) I was passing the house and just couldn't resist dropping in on you.

Ross I'm glad you did. But what are you doing in these parts?

Bill I've had a meeting with the people who tarted up *Toymaker*.

Ross Ah, yes! I remember your telling me about them. They're in Maidenhead.

Bill That's right. Devilishly clever people. But their accounts department! (*He shakes his head*) Ye gods!

Ross They can't add up, is that it?

Bill They can add up all right. It's getting them to subtract, that's the problem. Is Fay around?

Ross No, I'm afraid she isn't. Her sister's not well and she's looking after her. Did you wish to see Fay?

Bill It's just that — this morning, whilst I was having a shower, I suddenly had an idea. Get most of my ideas in the shower these days. It's a super idea, Ross. Just hope Fay will like it. And you too, of course.

Ross (*smiling*) What is this super idea, Bill?

Bill I have a villa in the south of France ...

Ross I know. We've seen photographs of it.

Bill So you have! Anyway, I thought it might be a good idea if Fay went down there for two or three weeks, or even longer if she feels like it. The house will be empty most of the summer — except for the couple who look after the place. Apart from anything else, Fay would be free of gossip, and it would give her a chance to, well — think things over.

Ross (*obviously approving of the suggestion*) Bill, you really are thoughtful! You must be the kindest person ——

Bill Now don't give me that bullshit, or I shall never take another shower.

Ross laughs

The ball's in your court. She'd like it down there, I'm sure. There's a super pool. Artificial waves, the lot.

Ross Bill, even if nothing comes of this, it's a very kind offer and I appreciate it.

Bill Well — put it to her. See what she says. (*He moves towards the terrace, then stops*) By the way, do you happen to know a young fellow called Gordon Black? He works for Campbell and Trasker, the textile people.

Ross Yes, I know him. He's Liz Kennedy's boyfriend—or rather, he was.

Bill That's the chap. He's thinking of buying a boat and last night, at Sam's suggestion, he came to see me. Bombarded me with all the usual questions: what would a boat cost, who were the best people to contact, etc., etc. Then he suddenly started talking about Liz. Don't quite know why, neither of us had mentioned her.

Ross What did he say about her?

Bill He said she was a really wonderful person and it was terrible what had happened to her.

Ross That sounds to me as if he's still fond of Liz.

Bill I think he is. In fact, I'm sure he is. After he left I did a spot of thinking ——

Ross In the shower?

Bill No — not in the shower this time. (*He hesitates*) This is none of my business, I realize that. So knock me down, Ross, if I'm talking out of turn.

Ross OK. I'll knock you down ...

Bill It's just that — I wondered whether it would be a good idea if Gordon paid Liz a visit? Took her out to lunch one day, perhaps ...

Ross I've thought of that. In fact I discussed it with Dr Lestrade who's looking after her. But it's still early days for Liz. The treatment's only just started.

Bill You're against the idea?

Ross We were. But in the light of what you've told me — maybe we should think again.

Bill I'm sure Gordon would co-operate.

Ross (*nodding*) I'll give it another thought.

Bill Incidentally, just as he was getting into his car he mentioned Julian.

Ross Gordon did?

Bill Yes. He'd read the obituaries and he wanted to know what I thought of Kane.

Ross Did you tell him?

Bill I evaded his questions. But not very well, I'm afraid.

Ross Did you ask him if he'd met Julian?

Bill Yes, I did. He said he hadn't, and I was the second person to ask that question.

Ross The second person? Who was he referring to, do you know?

Bill No, I'm afraid I don't.

They move toward the terrace

Talk to Fay about the villa, Ross. Don't let her turn the idea down.

Bill exits

Ross waves goodbye to Bill, then moves down to his desk. He stands for a second or two, hesitating, then he opens a drawer and takes out a London telephone directory. He consults the book, finds the number he is looking for, picks up the phone and dials

Ross (*into the phone*) Campbell and Trasker? ... My name is Marquand. Dr Marquand. Could I speak to Mr Gordon Black? ... Yes, of course. Thank you. ... Mr Black? ... This is Ross Marquand. We have met, but it was some little time ago. ... That's right. ... I'd very much like to see you, Mr Black, and I was wondering if we could meet? ... It's a little difficult over the phone. ... Well — as soon as possible. ... It so happens I'm in London this evening, perhaps you'd care to join me for a drink? ... Yes, seven o'clock would suit me very well. ... Shall we say the Garrick Club? ... Thank you, I shall look forward to seeing you. (*He hangs up. He stands by the phone, lost in thought*)

Judy enters, wearing outdoor clothes

Ross is momentarily unaware of her

Judy (*staring at him*) Ross ...

Ross (*turning*) Oh! Hallo, Judy ...

Judy You were miles away.

Ross Yes, I'm afraid I was.

An awkward pause. Judy is expecting Ross to question her

Judy Well?
Ross (*tersely*) Well — what?
Judy Aren't you going to ask me what happened?

Ross stares at her, blankly

I've just come back from Harley Street. There was a crisis, remember? You asked me to deal with it.
Ross Yes. Yes, of course. I'm sorry. What happened?
Judy The builders discovered there was dry rot behind one of the beams and there was panic all round. Anyway, I've sorted it out. Another firm is dealing with it. All being well they'll start work ... first ... thing on ... (*She stops*)

Judy realizes that Ross is not listening to her

What is it, Ross? I don't believe you've heard a word I've said!
Ross (*urgently; almost as if coming to life*) What are my appointments tomorrow?
Judy Your appointments?
Ross Yes! My appointments!
Judy You've got a fairly easy day. You're seeing Mrs Crayford at ten o'clock. Professor Hope-Stanway at eleven, Mr and Mrs Drayton at——
Ross (*with quick irritation; stopping her*) How many appointments, Judy? That's all I want to know.
Judy Er — four in the morning. Two in the afternoon. And I've arranged for you to see the builder at six o'clock.
Ross Cancel the appointments and tell the builder I'll see him one day next week.
Judy (*taken aback*) Cancel the appointments?
Ross Yes.
Judy All of them?
Ross All of them! I shan't be here tomorrow. I'm taking the day off.

He quickly exits into the hall

Judy stares after him, completely lost for words

Black-out

SCENE 5

The same. Late the following evening

Fay is on the telephone endeavouring to bring a lengthy conversation to a close

Fay (*into the phone*) Yes, Marian, I know the restaurant. We've been there before. ... I'm sure we have. ... I can't remember when, Marian, but I know we've been there. ... Well, not to worry, I'll find it. (*She attempts to hang up*) One o'clock, I'll be there. ... All right, Marian, we'll meet at the boutique if that would suit you better. ... Absolutely. ... One o'clock. ... Twelve-thirty? ... Yes, all right, twelve-thirty. ... (*With good-natured exasperation*) Marian, I *know* where the boutique is! See you tomorrow ... (*She hangs up*)

She crosses to the sofa. There is the sound of the front door closing. She turns to the hall

   Ross enters. He looks weary but immediately brightens up at the sight of Fay

Ross Why, hallo, Fay!

Fay Where have you been, Ross? I wondered what had happened to you. No-one seemed to know where you were or what you were doing.

Ross (*evasively*) I'm sorry, Fay. I should have phoned you.

Fay I understand from Judy you cancelled today's appointments?

Ross Yes.

Fay That's not like you, Ross.

Ross It was unfortunate, but it just couldn't be helped.

Fay Aren't you well?

Ross Yes. I'm well. (*Deliberately changing the subject*) How's your sister? Is she better?

Fay (*staring at him; puzzled*) Yes, she is. So much so, she insisted I come home.

Ross That's good news. I'm delighted. When did you get back?

Fay About an hour ago.

Pause

Ross Is Judy around?

Fay No. She's out. You've just missed her. She's having dinner with Alan.

Ross (*crossing to the desk*) I'm sorry you were not here yesterday afternoon. Bill dropped by. He was hoping to see you.

Fay Bill?

Ross Yes. He's come up with an idea, or rather, a suggestion. A very good one, I think. (*Pause*) He has a house in the South of France ...

Fay Yes, I know.

Ross It's going to be empty for most of the summer and he's suggested you might like to go down there for two or three weeks — longer if you felt like it. There's a couple living in so you'd be well looked-after. (*Slight pause*) What do you think of the idea?

Pause

Fay It's very kind of Bill.

Ross Yes, it is. Very. (*Pause*) Have you thought of going away?

Fay Yes, I have. I told you. Diana suggested we go on a cruise together, but I've seen rather a lot of my sister recently and right now I'd like to be on my own. For a time at any rate ...

Ross I can understand that.

Pause

Fay What did you tell Bill?

Ross I said I'd talk to you.

Pause

Fay I'm tempted, Ross. But I'd like to think about it.

Ross Yes, of course. You do that, Fay, and let me know what you decide.

Fay nods and, seemingly lost in thought, moves slowly towards the hall. Then suddenly she stops and turns towards Ross again

Fay If I accepted Bill's offer ... do you think you could take a few days off ... so that we could drive down to Menton?

Ross Why, yes! Yes, of course, Fay!

Fay I've never been keen on flying, you know that.

Ross I'd be happy, more than happy, to drive you down there.

Fay Then we'll talk about it later.

She exits

Pause. Ross, obviously pleased by Fay's suggestion, turns his attention to a pile of unopened letters on his desk. He starts to open one of them

Fay enters with Sam

Fay Sam's here, Ross.

Ross (*turning*) Oh, hallo, Sam! You obviously got my message. Good!

Sam I'm sorry I was out when you phoned.

Ross That's all right. (*He puts the letter down*) You're here, that's the main thing. (*To Fay*) Thank you, Fay.

Fay Bye, Sam.

Sam Goodbye, Fay. See you again soon, I hope.

Fay exits

Ross Sit down, Sam. I'll get you a drink.

Sam No, thank you, Ross.

Ross Well — do you mind if I have one? (*He crosses to the cabinet*) I've had rather a tiring day. I've only just got back from Scotland. (*He begins to pour himself a drink*)

Sam What were you doing in Scotland?

Ross As a matter of fact, I went to see your daughter.

Sam (*taken aback*) Liz? Is that why you wanted to see me? (*His alarm bells are ringing*) What's happened, Ross? Is she worse? Did Dr Lestrade send for you?

Ross No-one sent for me and Liz is getting along well, all things considered. Just relax, Sam. (*Pause. He continues fixing his drink*) Look — are you sure you won't have one?

Sam Yes, I'm quite sure.

Ross Well — sit down.

Sam, obviously still a shade worried, puts his case down and sits in one of the armchairs. Pause

Sam There's something on your mind, Ross. What is it?

Ross, drink in hand, moves to the settee and sits on the arm

Ross I'm afraid I owe you an apology. I did something last night which I shouldn't have done without first consulting you. (*He drinks*) I met Gordon. Liz's ex-boyfriend. I talked to him for the best part of an hour.
Sam That's all right. That doesn't call for an apology ...
Ross Liz is your daughter, not mine. I really had no right to question Gordon about her.
Sam That's nonsense, Ross! If your talking to Gordon, or anyone else for that matter, will help Liz, then for heaven's sake talk your head off. But why see Gordon?
Ross I wanted to find out what his present feelings were towards Liz. Whether he was still fond of her.
Sam And did you find out?
Ross Yes, I did. He said in the past he'd proposed to Liz, more than once. And in spite of recent events he still wanted to marry her.
Sam (*shaking his head; with a note of despair*) I love my daughter, but there are times when I think that young man is far too good for her.
Ross It was after seeing Gordon that I went to the clinic. I told Liz what had happened and for the first time — the very first time — she was prepared to talk. (*He drinks, then puts the glass down*) By the time I left she was not only talking to me, she was on the phone to Gordon.
Sam This is wonderful news, Ross! Janet will be thrilled ——
Ross Whether things will work out for them, I don't honestly know. But it won't be Gordon's fault if they don't. I'm sure of that.

Pause

Sam You say Liz talked? What did she talk about? Herself?
Ross Yes. And she was surprisingly frank. She answered all my questions. Well — nearly all of them.
Sam Did she explain about the drug situation? How she came to be on heroin?
Ross She met a man — a celebrity — at the Barbican and fell completely under his spell. She was besotted by him. That's the only way you can

describe it. She was convinced he was serious about her, which wasn't the case. He was merely amusing himself. When the truth dawned on Liz she became desperate, suicidal. A so-called friend persuaded her to try heroin. The rest we know.

Pause

Sam This man — this man she fell for — did she tell you who he was?

Ross No. But she didn't have to. I knew who it was. It was Julian Kane.

Sam (*taken aback*) Julian? Are you sure?

Ross Last night, before going to Scotland, I visited the Barbican. I made inquiries about Julian and I discovered that his first concert there coincided with the disappearance of your daughter. (*Pause*) I also discovered something else, Sam. I discovered that you too had been making inquiries about Julian.

Sam Me?

Ross Yes, and not only at the Barbican. You questioned Gordon about him. You wanted to know if Gordon knew Julian. Whether Liz had ever mentioned him.

Sam My dear chap, I'd never set eyes on Kane until you introduced him to me on the terrace that morning.

Ross I know that, Sam.

Sam (*rising from the chair*) Then what are you suggesting?

Ross I'm suggesting that your friend Dr Thornton was wrong and that Julian was not on Zarabell. I'm suggesting that at some point during the morning one of us — one of our party, that is — deliberately gave Julian a drink with Zarabell in it. And that's what killed him.

Sam But aren't you forgetting something? What about the phial he had in his pocket? Apart from the fact that it was on his person the phial was in a silver box which had Julian's initials on it. That proved to the coroner, and everyone else, that Julian had been taking the drug. Dash it all, Ross, you saw the box!

Ross Yes, I saw it. But the box could have been planted on Julian.

Sam Planted on him? How on earth could anyone have put the box in his pocket without him knowing?

Ross You've asked a simple question. So I'll give you a simple answer. *You* could have planted it on him. *You* could have put it in his pocket.

Sam I could? When? On the terrace, in front of everybody?

Ross No. Not on the terrace. You could have placed it in his pocket *after* he'd had the heart attack.

Sam (*puzzled*) After the heart attack? I'm sorry, but I'm not with you ...

Ross (*quietly*) I think you are. (*Pause*) Do I have to spell it out? (*Pause*) You planted the box on Julian whilst you examined him. You did it here! Right here, in this room! (*Pause*) I recognized the box. It was your wife's. Some time back Janet consulted me and I gave her some pills. She put them in the box she was using. A silver box with her initials on it. J.K. Janet Kennedy ...

There is a strained, uncomfortable silence between them. Then a somewhat shaken Sam moves across to the window and stands staring out at the terrace. A long pause

Well, Sam?

Sam (*slowly turning*) Julian Kane was a monster! The unhappiness that man caused was quite unbelievable. You can't begin to imagine the number of lives he ruined. He would never have left Liz alone. That just wasn't his way. Sooner or later he'd have entered her life again. I'm sure of that. Absolutely sure!

Ross (*his eyes on Sam*) So you killed him?

Sam Yes, and believe me, given the same circumstances I'd do it again!

Ross Would you, Sam?

Sam Yes, I would.

Ross No regrets?

Sam None.

Ross No sleepless nights? No nightmares?

Sam (*adamant; totally convincing*) None! None whatsoever! (*He smiles*) No side effects, Ross. Definitely no side effects!

Ross Does anyone else know what happened? Have you confided in anyone?

Sam No. No-one knows, except you. (*Pause. With obvious sincerity*) We've been colleagues and friends for a long time, and I've always been proud of that, Ross. So I'm sorry, terribly sorry, that you should have discovered what happened that morning. However, believe me, I understand ——

Ross What is it you understand, Sam?

Sam I understand that you must be free to do what you think is best.

Ross Even if it means talking to our friend Sanders?

Pause

Sam Yes, even if it means talking to Sanders.

The two men gaze at each other steadily

  Sam picks up his case, turns quickly and exits

After a long pause Ross gets his drink and, deep in thought, moves down to the cabinet. He stands for quite a while, slowly drinking, his thoughts obviously on Sam. Suddenly a look of determination appears on his face. Putting down his glass, he crosses to the telephone but simply stands staring down at it. He looks like a man trying desperately hard to reach a decision. Finally, and still uncertain of himself, he picks up the phone and dials

Ross (*into the phone*) This is Dr Marquand. ... Is Chief Inspector Sanders available? ... Yes, I'll hold ... (*Pause. Suddenly, impulsively, he changes his mind and slams down the receiver*)

Visibly shaken, he returns to the cabinet, finishes his drink, and prepares to fix himself another one. He has completed this task when the phone rings. He turns, startled. The phone continues ringing. After a little while, he can no longer stand it and moves to the phone. Pause. He picks up the phone

  (*Into the phone*) Oh, hallo, Inspector. ... Yes, I did phone you. There was something I wanted to ...(*his expression and manner suddenly change. He has finally reached a decision and now, once again, he is the self-assured consultant*) It was just that I wanted to make sure you'd started on the medication. ... You have? ... Good! ... That's correct, four a day — and don't forget the one at bedtime, so many patients do. ... What's that? ... (*An appreciable pause*) Don't worry about that, my dear fellow! Put it completely out of your head. (*Almost as if speaking to himself*) There'll be no side effects, I assure you ...

The Lights quickly fade

CURTAIN

FURNITURE AND PROPERTY LIST

ACT I
SCENE 1

On stage: Armchairs
Sofa
Drinks cabinet with glasses and bottles of scotch
Centre table
Ashtray
Impressive-looking desk. *On it:* telephone, notebooks, stationery,
    pens, letterknife, etc.
Desk chair
Telephone directory in desk drawer
Drink (for **Alan**)
Canvas holdall (for **Alan**)

Personal: **Judy:** wrist-watch (worn throughout)

SCENE 2

Strike: Drink

Set: Vase of yellow roses on table

Off stage: Briefcase (**Sam**)
Scarf (**Fay**)

Personal: **Ross:** wrist-watch (worn throughout)
Sam: wrist-watch (worn throughout)

SCENE 3

Off stage: Letters and document (**Judy**)
Cardboard box containing a phial (**Judy**)

SCENE 4

Strike: Vase of roses

Set: Cardboard box in desk drawer
                Gold cigarette lighter on table

Off stage: Oily rag (**Alan**)
                Glass of wine (**Julian**)
                Cigarette (**Marian**)
                Tray with empty glasses (**Judy**)
                Raincoat (**Fay**)

Personal: **Ross:** phial in pocket

ACT II
Scene 1

Off stage: Deck of cards (**Bill**)

Personal: **Alan:** gun in pocket

Scene 2

Set: **Sam's** briefcase

Scene 3

No props

Scene 4

Off stage: Overcoat and hat (**Sanders**)

Personal: **Marian:** handbag with mirror

Scene 5

Set: Pile of letters on desk

Off stage: Briefcase (**Sam**)

LIGHTING PLOT

Interior. Same setting throughout
Practical fittings required: standard lamp

ACT I, SCENE 1

To open: Bring up late afternoon effect

Cue 1   **Alan** heads towards the open window   (Page 7)
          Fade to black-out

ACT I, SCENE 2

To open: Bring up night effect

Cue 2   **Ross:** "... a man called Julian Kane ..."   (Page 18)
          Fade to black-out

ACT I, SCENE 3

To open: Bring up afternoon effect

Cue 3   **Ross** stares at the phial   (Page 26)
          Fade to black-out

ACT I, SCENE 4

To open: Bring up morning effect: sunshine with gathering clouds

Cue 4   **Julian** stands staring up at the sky   (Page 40)
          Flash of lightning

Cue 5   **Fay** stares at **Ross**   (Page 41)
          Fade to black-out

ACT II, SCENE 1

To open: Bring up night effect

Cue 6   **Judy** tears up the note   (Page 54)
              Black-out

ACT II, SCENE 2

To open: Bring up afternoon effect

Cue 7   **Ross:** "Thank you, Fay."   (Page 61)
              Fade to black-out

ACT II, SCENE 3

To open: Bring up late afternoon effect

Cue 8   **Bill:** "Well — hardly ever."   (Page 65)
              Fade to black-out

ACT II, SCENE 4

To open: Bring up sunny afternoon effect

Cue 9   **Judy** stares after **Ross**   (Page 75)
              Black-out

ACT II, SCENE 5

To open: Bring up late evening effect

Cue 10   **Ross:** "... I assure you ..."   (Page 81)
              Fade to black-out

EFFECTS PLOT

ACT I

Cue 1	**Judy:** "It probably would." *Telephone rings*	(Page 2)
Cue 2	To open Scene 2 *Doorbell*	(Page 7)
Cue 3	**Ross:** "He's a personal research consultant." *Sound of a door closing*	(Page 14)
Cue 4	**Ross:** "We'd better keep them in here." *Telephone rings*	(Page 25)
Cue 5	To open Scene 4 *Sound of a party in progress (throughout the scene)*	(Page 26)
Cue 6	**Ross:** "And the forecast isn't good." *Distant roll of thunder*	(Page 26)
Cue 7	Flash of lightning *Long roll of thunder*	(Page 40)

ACT II

Cue 8	To open Scene 1 *Telephone rings*	(Page 42)
Cue 9	**Judy:** "Yes, of course." *Sound of a car horn*	(Page 47)
Cue 10	**Judy** moves towards the consulting room *Doorbell. Pause. Doorbell again*	(Page 50)
Cue 11	**Judy** exits into the hall *Sound of a door opening*	(Page 50)

MADE AND PRINTED IN GREAT BRITAIN BY
LATIMER TREND & COMPANY LTD PLYMOUTH
MADE IN ENGLAND